A TRIBUTE TO
BASIL BERNSTEIN
1924–2000

A TRIBUTE TO
BASIL BERNSTEIN
1924–2000

Edited by
Sally Power, Peter Aggleton, Julia Brannen, Andrew Brown,
Lynne Chisholm and John Mace

INSTITUTE OF
EDUCATION
UNIVERSITY OF LONDON

First published in 2001 by the Institute of Education, University of London, 20 Bedford Way, London WC1H 0AL
www.ioe.ac.uk

Pursuing Excellence in Education

© Institute of Education, University of London 2001

British Library Cataloguing in Publication Data:
A catalogue record for this publication is available from the British Library

ISBN 0 85473 651 4

Extract from *Duino Elegies* by Rainer Maria Rilke, translated by J. B. Leishman and Stephen Spender, published by Hogarth Press. Used by permission of St John's College Oxford and the Random House Group Ltd. 'Mending Wall' from *The Poetry of Robert Frost*, edited by Edward Connery Lathem, used by permission of the Estate of Robert Frost and Jonathan Cape (the Random House Group Ltd) publishers. 'Aubade' from *Collected Poems* of Philip Larkin, edited by Anthony Thwaite, used by permission of Faber and Faber Ltd.

Cover photograph © Francis Bernstein

Designed by Tim McPhee
Page make-up by Cambridge Photosetting Services, Cambridge
Production Services by
Book Production Consultants plc, Cambridge
Printed by Watkiss Studios, Biggleswade

CONTENTS

Part 2 Letters

Part 3 Written Tributes

CONTENTS

EDITORS' FOREWORD

BASIL BERNSTEIN WAS ONE of the most eminent sociologists of the past 30 years. His work focused on education and cultural transmissions but has much wider relevance. His death in September 2000 was not just a tragic loss for all those who knew him, but also for the academic world. For the Institute of Education in particular his death ended a long and highly productive relationship in which he made an outstanding contribution to theory and research and inspired the intellectual development of individual staff and students.

On hearing the sad news of his death, the Director put in place arrangements to honour Basil Bernstein's contribution to the academic community. As part of this, an organising committee was established to arrange a memorial event that would bring together those people for whom his work had particular resonance. In planning the day, it very quickly became clear to the committee that it would be impossible to give a platform to all of those who would like to contribute. In selecting our speakers, we wanted to reflect the breadth of academic areas to which Basil's work contributed, the international audience to whom he spoke and his inspirational work with research students. We were delighted that several hundred people were able to attend – many of them having travelled thousands of miles. The list of countries represented at the event includes Australia, Chile, Greece, Japan, Portugal and the USA, to name but a few. However, the spoken tributes presented on the day reflect only a small selection of those we received – many of those who were unable to speak or attend provided us with written tributes which are also included in this collection.

The book is organised into three sections. The programme of the proceedings of the day and the spoken contributions are presented in section 1 (which also includes an unanticipated but welcome 'Homage from Chile' brought in person by Christian Cox). Section 2 contains a selection of the many messages and letters we received. Section 3 contains, in alphabetical order, the written tributes.

We hope this tribute illustrates the very great esteem in which Basil was held – both personally and professionally – and the continuing importance of his scholarship around the globe.

Peter Aggleton
Julia Brannen
Andrew Brown
Lynne Chisholm
John Mace
Sally Power

PART ONE

THE SYMPOSIUM

PROGRAMME
Basil Bernstein: A Celebration of his Life and Work

Morning Session: Logan Hall

11.00   Sir William Taylor, Former Director, Institute of Education
Welcome

11.05   *Music:* Catherine Edwards (piano)
Prelude and Fugue in E flat minor, Book 1, Johann Sebastian Bach

11.15   Professor Geoff Whitty, Director, Institute of Education
'*A Personal and Institutional Tribute to Basil Bernstein*'

11.30   Professor Alan Sadovnik, Rutgers University
'*Basil Bernstein: Sociologist of Education and Mentor*'

11.45   *Music:* Peter Hayward (counter tenor), Stavria Kotsoni-Brown (cello)
and Catherine Edwards (piano)

Three songs:
Dove sei
From Rodelinda, George Frederick Handel

Esurientes
From the Magnificat, Johann Sebastian Bach

An Evening Hymn
Henry Purcell, words by Dr William Fuller, late Lord Bishop of
Lincoln

11.55   *Poetry reading:* Professor Julia Brannen, Institute of Education

12.05   Professor Ana Morais, University of Lisbon
'*Crossing Boundaries between Disciplines: A Perspective on Basil
Bernstein's Legacy*'

12.20   Professor Paul Atkinson, University of Cardiff
'*Basil Bernstein's Legacy to Sociology*'

12.45   *Music:* Catherine Edwards (piano) and Stavria Kotsoni-Brown (cello)
Sonata no. 4, Vivaldi

13.00   Wine reception and buffet (Jeffery Hall)
         Toastmaster: Sir William Taylor

Afternoon Session: Logan Hall

14.15   Professor Stephen Ball, Karl Mannheim Professor Designate,
         Institute of Education
         Introduction to the afternoon

14.20   PD Dr habil Lynne Chisholm, European Commission DG
         Education and Culture
         *'Thinking about Education and Power in Knowledge Societies –
         What are the Implications of Contemporary Social Change?'*

14.40   **Panel discussion:**
         *'The Diverse Influence of Basil Bernstein's Work and Lines of
         Future Development'*

         Moderator: Professor Harry Daniels, University of Birmingham

         Panel Members:
         Professor Bill Hillier, Bartlett Graduate School, University College
         London
         Professor Courtney Cazden, Harvard Graduate School of Education
         Professor Gunther Kress, Institute of Education
         Dr Madeleine Arnot, University of Cambridge

15.20   Dr Andrew Brown, Institute of Education
         *'Becoming a Researcher: Reflections on the Pedagogic Practices of
         Basil Bernstein'*

15.35   Professor Fred Inglis, Sheffield University
         *'Elaborating Bernstein: The Pedagogic Devices of a Great
         Sociologist'*

15.50   Announcements

16.00   **Close**

INTRODUCTION

Professor Sir William Taylor CBE, Director of the
Institute of Education 1973–1983

Ladies and Gentlemen

We come together today to celebrate the achievements of a man who, directly
or indirectly, has touched the professional lives of all of us, not only in this
hall, not only in the Institute more generally, but wherever men and women
engage in education as teachers, as researchers and as learners.

This is, as the programme makes clear, a celebration. But it is fitting at the
outset that we recognise that with us this morning are a number of people for
whom Basil's passing has been much more than the loss of a distinguished
colleague, an esteemed teacher, a major contributor to sociological theory, a
critical and challenging friend. I refer of course to Marion Bernstein and to
members of her family.

To you, Marion, may we extend our condolences on your grievous loss,
and express our thanks for all you did over so many years to support and to
sustain Basil's professional life, and by so doing to enable all of us, in this hall
and beyond, to benefit from the great contributions he made to education and
to sociology.

May I ask that we stand for a moment in silent fellowship to pay our
personal tributes to Basil and to express our commiserations to Marion and
to all the other members of his family, both present and afar.

Thank you

During this morning and afternoon some of Basil's colleagues and former
students will be telling us something about his work in sociology and in
education. As we shall hear, he has left an indelible mark on studies in these
fields. Most of his professional work was undertaken while he was a member

of staff of this Institute. Great universities in other countries would have been proud to have him on their faculties. But it was to the Institute that he gave his professional and his personal allegiance.

It is fitting therefore, that it is in the Institute that this celebration should take place. In planning the day, it has also been the intention to emphasise Basil's enduring love of the arts. He enjoyed a deep appreciation and knowledge of music, contemporary art and fine literature. In important ways his intellectual work and aesthetic sense complemented and nourished each other.

Thus today's programme includes music and poetry as well as tributes to Basil's academic work, all of which reflect the sensibilities of the man himself.

A PERSONAL AND INSTITUTIONAL TRIBUTE TO BASIL BERNSTEIN

*Geoff Whitty, Director of the Institute of Education,
University of London*

BASIL BERNSTEIN HAD A huge influence on this Institute from the 1960s until his death last year. In formal terms, you could say that, as Senior Lecturer, Reader, Professor, Karl Mannheim Professor, Head of Department, Pro-Director and finally Emeritus Professor he worked here under six Directors, but the notion of Basil working *under* anyone is more than faintly ludicrous. None of us could aspire even to be his peer. Nevertheless, as current Director I am delighted to have the honour of speaking at today's memorial event. I am also pleased that three former Directors, Bill Taylor, Denis Lawton and Peter Mortimore, are present with us today. Unfortunately, neither Lionel Elvin nor Peter Newsam has been able to join us, but both wish they could have done. Lionel Elvin, who was the Director who appointed Basil, told me that 'like Freud, Basil Bernstein put into circulation concepts that entered into the general stream of professional consciousness.... It was always not only profitable but a pleasure to talk to him about this work. He was indeed one of the chief ornaments of the Institute.' Peter Newsam, who (in a sense) was the Director Basil appointed, told me that 'It was Basil who first approached me about coming to the Institute. He was the dominant intellectual force when I was here; he was known all around the world.'

I am sure that all the former Directors would agree with me that, at the same time as being a major figure on the world intellectual stage in sociology and socio-linguistics, Basil has been responsible, more than any other individual, for the Institute's present-day standing as a major centre of research and scholarship. His Sociological Research Unit became part of the Social

Science Research Unit, and he was also instrumental in the founding of the Multi-Cultural Education Centre, which has grown into the International Centre for Intercultural Studies. These and many other aspects of Institute life will continue to be testimony to his influence. But, although today is about celebrating Basil's life and work and its continuing influence, there is still a tangible sense of sadness and loss around the place now that our greatest scholar is no longer with us in person.

Like many other people here today, I also feel a considerable sense of personal loss. Basil directly touched the lives of generations of staff and students at the Institute. In my own case, he inspired me to a follow a path I would never have contemplated before coming under his spell. And I can date the moment exactly: to a lecture in the Beveridge Hall on 11 October 1968 when I was a PGCE student here. Basil inspired me far more than anyone had succeeded in doing during my undergraduate degree and has been a pervasive influence on my own academic life ever since. I can still conjure up in my mind his words, his presence on the stage and his mannerisms while delivering his lectures. And, although over years I have struggled with the depth and richness of many of his more difficult concepts and ideas, it was actually a very simple statement on that particular day in 1968 which was the Road to Damascus moment that turned me into a sociologist of the curriculum.

Before Basil's lecture that day, there would have been another contribution, from a philosopher, probably on education as an intrinsically worthwhile activity or on forms of knowledge as the basis for the curriculum, but I have no recollection of either the form or the content of that contribution. Then it was Basil's turn. Coming to the front of the stage, he said 'just for a moment forget what you've just heard and forget what is actually in the school curriculum you're going to teach year in year out for the next however many years. Just think of it as a series of empty units of time spread through the week. Then ask yourselves why and how some things come to fill up those units and not others. Why – he said in a characteristic aside – is poetry in there and not pornography? And why do some subjects, like maths, get all the good slots, while general studies gets left with the dregs on Friday after-noons. And why are some subjects kept apart with strong barriers between them and others allowed to permeate each other in time and space...'

Those words from Basil broke through my taken-for-granted assumptions about school knowledge. In a paper circulating the following year, he wrote: 'there is nothing intrinsic about how educational time is used, or the status of the various contents or the relation between the contents. I am emphasising the social nature of the system of choices from which emerges a constellation called a curriculum.' The same basic idea underlies both forms of the statement, but it was Basil's qualities as a teacher as well as a thinker that changed the way I understood school knowledge. Without that moment of brilliant teaching, even though I could later have read the same basic idea and the rest of the lecture on collection and integrated codes in its brilliant elaboration in the various chapters of *Class, Codes and Control, Volume 3* – incidentally still one of the most well-thumbed books on my shelves – I doubt whether I would ever have gone on to study sociology of education at the Institute in the 1970s. To then eventually have had the honour of succeeding Basil as the Karl Mannheim Professor was beyond my dreams and I was delighted that he was in the audience when I gave the Karl Mannheim Memorial Lecture in 1997 – even if I didn't say enough about Durkheim for his liking! And he was on brilliant form when he and Marion joined the celebratory dinner hosted by Peter Mortimore after that lecture.

Although I was never as close to Basil personally as some other people here, we kept in touch right from our first meeting in the late1960s until the last time I saw him at his home in Dulwich last August. That first face-to-face meeting was when a group of us rather bolshie PGCE students, veterans of May 1968, went to see him in his office in Taviton Street to demand to know how he could possibly justify the Institute's hierarchical examination system given the sorts of things that he was writing. He immediately took us for a lunchtime drink – the first of many I had with Basil over the years. He charmed us out of our aggression and gave us an impromptu lecture on the role of the intellectual in society. Only later did I realize that much of it was at least tongue in cheek and that, to some extent, he was playing with us. But it did the trick. In fact, of course, Basil was by no means the sort of dispassionate intellectual he made himself out to be on that occasion. Witness, for example, his later role in the founding of the Centre for Multi-Cultural Education here, wherein rigorous analysis and passionate commitment came together in the struggle for racial justice.

I got to know Basil a little better when I became an MA student here in 1972. In that context, he was not performing on the Beveridge Hall stage in front of a large audience, but sitting on the floor in a Gordon Square seminar room, often using an unlit cigarette to emphasize his point and occasionally jumping up to scribble a diagrammatic representation of his ideas on the board, then retiring to the Marlborough with us to continue the discussion. After I left the Institute, I used to meet up with Basil for lunch from time to time and when I eventually came back to the Institute in 1992, we tried to lunch together at least once a term. These lunchtime occasions nearly always took the same form. Twenty or thirty minutes of Basil's sheer intellectual brilliance on whatever we were discussing, usually illustrated diagrammatically on whatever was to hand, most usually paper napkins, of which I still have quite a collection. I know others have their own collections, so we might even publish them some day. Once that work was done, we would eat and drink, others would often join us and then his incisive wit would come into full play, often (of course) at my own expense!

Everyone has their favourite Basil stories. People sit in bars all over the world exchanging them. I will tell just one today, because I think it shows the different sides of Basil that I have encountered over the years and because it would hardly be true to his memory to pretend that he was always easy to deal with. It comes from the time when I was at King's in the early 1980s. One of my PhD students and I had written a paper that drew on some of Basil's ideas. I sent him a draft for comment and got a very angry phone call in return which ended with him saying he blamed the supervisor, deploring the sad decline in academic standards at King's and slamming the phone down. Needless to say, I was rather upset, not least because his whole argument seemed to turn on our having missed the import of footnote 157 in a so far unpublished revision of a paper we had cited. After fretting for hours about the sheer unreasonableness of his attack, I plucked up the courage to call him at home that evening. Nervous as I was, it was the right thing to do. The call lasted nearly an hour, the first twenty minutes were difficult to say the least, but it then miraculously transformed into a serious intellectual engagement about the actual matter in question. It produced a better paper on our part and I treated the whole incident as a rite of passage and really forgot about it. Some time later, when the student had been awarded his PhD, we all went out to dinner. Basil ordered an expensive bottle of wine and, as it was being poured, he said to us with a smile, 'this is by way of a silly old man saying he's sorry'. How can you *not* love someone like that? And, infuriating as he certainly *could* be, there were many more occasions when he was a delight to be with and when he offered me personal support as well as academic inspiration. I will always remember that with gratitude.

Basil has left us with ways of looking *at* the world and being *in* the world that will influence us for years to come. I am delighted that the Institute has been able to celebrate his life and work in this way today and the numbers here are indicative of the tremendous respect and affection in which he is held. The last time I saw Basil, we were discussing a possible event in which we hoped he himself would be able to participate, at least on video. Although it was not to be, it gave me some ideas about the sort of occasion he would have wanted us to hold – one which not only recognizes his own immense achievements but also explores ways of building on them in the future. That was really the only guidance I gave the organizing committee and I can see that they have not only acted on that but also included many other things he himself would have appreciated. I would like to thank them personally, on behalf of the Institute and, I am sure, on behalf of Basil himself.

BASIL BERNSTEIN (1924–2000)

Sociologist, mentor and friend

Alan R. Sadovnik, Rutgers University, New Jersey, USA

FOR OVER FOUR DECADES, Bernstein was a centrally important and controversial sociologist, whose work has influenced a generation of sociologists of education and linguists. From his early works on language, communication codes and schooling, to his later works on pedagogic discourse, practice and educational transmissions, Bernstein attempted to produce a theory of social and educational codes and their effect on social reproduction. Although structuralist in its approach, Bernstein's sociology has drawn on the essential theoretical orientations in the field – Durkheimian, Weberian, Marxist and interactionist – and provides the possibility of an important synthesis. Primarily, he viewed his work as most heavily influenced by Durkheim.

Karabel and Halsey (1977: 62), in their review of the literature on the sociology of education, called Bernstein's work the 'harbinger of a new synthesis', a view entirely justified by subsequent events. Bernstein's early work on code theory was highly controversial, as it discussed social-class differences in language, which some labelled a deficit theory, but it nonetheless raised crucial questions about the relationships among the social division of labour, the family and the school, and explored how these relationships affected differences in learning among the social classes. His later work (1977a) began the difficult project of connecting macro-power and class relations to the micro-educational processes of the school. Whereas class reproduction theorists, such as Bowles and Gintis (1976), offered an overtly deterministic view of schools without describing or explaining what goes on in schools, Bernstein's work promised to connect the societal, institutional, interactional and intra-psychic levels of sociological analysis. In doing so, it presented an opportunity to synthesize the classical theoretical traditions of the discipline: Marxist, Weberian and Durkheimian.

Bernstein's early work on language (1958, 1960, 1961 a and b) examined the relationship between public language, authority and shared meanings (Danzig 1995: 146–7). By 1962, Bernstein began the development of code theory through the introduction of the concepts of restricted and elaborated codes (1962a, 1962b). In *Class, Codes and Control, Volume 1* (1973a), Bernstein's sociolinguistic code theory was developed into a social theory examining the relationships between social class, family and the reproduction of meaning systems (code refers to the principles regulating meaning systems). For Bernstein, there were social-class differences in the communication codes of working-class and middle-class children; differences that reflect the class and power relations in the social division of labour, family and schools. Based upon empirical research, Bernstein distinguished between the restricted code of the working class and the elaborated code of the middle class. Restricted codes are context dependent and particularistic, whereas elaborated codes are context independent and universalistic. For example, working-class boys asked to tell a story describing a series of pictures used many pronouns and their story could only be understood by looking at the pictures. Middle-class boys, on the other hand, generated descriptions rich in nouns and their story could be understood without the benefit of the pictures (Bernstein 1970). Although Bernstein's critics (see Danzig 1995) argued that his sociolinguistic theory represented an example of deficit theory, as they alleged that he was arguing that working-class language was deficient, Bernstein has consistently rejected this interpretation (see Bernstein 1996: 147–56). Bernstein has argued that restricted codes are not deficient, but rather are functionally related to the social division of labour, where context-dependent language is necessary in the context of production. Likewise, the elaborated code of the middle classes represents functional changes necessitated by changes in the division of labour and the middle classes' new position in reproduction, rather than production. That schools require an elaborated code for success means that working-class children are disadvantaged by the dominant code of schooling, not deficient. For Bernstein, difference becomes deficit in the context of macro-power relations.

By the third volume of *Class, Codes and Control* (1977a), Bernstein developed code theory from its sociolinguistic roots to examine the connection between communication codes and pedagogic discourse and practice. In this respect, code theory became concerned with the processes of schooling and how they related to social class reproduction. Bernstein's quest for understanding the microprocesses of schooling led him to continue to pursue the fruitful avenue of inquiry developed in his article 'Class and pedagogies: visible and invisible' (1977b). In that article, Bernstein analysed the significant differences between two generic forms of educational transmission and suggested that the differences in the classification and framing rules of each pedagogic practice (VP-visible = strong classification and strong framing; IP-invisible = weak classification and weak framing)' relate to the social-class position and assumptions of the families served by the schools. Classification refers to relations between categories regarding the social division of labour and is related to the distribution of power. Framing refers to the location of control over the rules of communication. (For a detailed analysis of this aspect of Bernstein's work, see Atkinson 1985; Atkinson, Davies and Delamont 1995; Sadovnik 1991, 1995.) The article clearly demonstrated that sociologists of education had to do the difficult empirical work of looking into the world of schools and of linking educational practices to the larger institutional, societal and historical factors of which they are a part.

Over the past 25 years, Bernstein developed this approach into a systematic analysis of pedagogic discourse and practices. First, he outlined a theory of pedagogic rules that examines the 'intrinsic features which constitute and distinguish the specialized form of communication realized by the pedagogic discourse of education' (1986/1990d: 165). Second (1990b), he related his theory of pedagogic discourse to a social-class base and applied it to the ongoing development of different educational practices.

The concept of code is central to Bernstein's structural sociology. From the outset of its use in his work on language (restricted and elaborated codes), code refers to a 'regulative principle which underlies various message systems, especially curriculum and pedagogy' (Atkinson 1985: 136). Curriculum and pedagogy are considered message systems and with a third system, evaluation, they constitute the structure and processes of school knowledge, transmission and practice. As Bernstein (1973b: 85) noted: 'Curriculum defines what counts as valid knowledge, pedagogy defines what counts as valid transmission of knowledge, and evaluation defines what counts as a valid realization of the knowledge on the part of the taught.' Thus, his theory of curriculum must be understood in terms of the concepts of classification, framing and evaluation, and their relationship to the structural aspects of his sociological project.

Bernstein's major earlier work on curriculum is contained in two important articles, 'On the classification and framing of educational knowledge' (1973b) and 'Class and pedagogies: visible and invisible' (1977b). The first article outlined the concepts of classification and framing and related them to an overall structuralist theory of curriculum and pedagogic practice. The second extended this analysis by applying it to the evolution of organic solidarity and to changes in the dynamics of production and social-class reproduction. It is this latter article of which Bernstein's later work on pedagogic practice is an extension. To understand the evolution of his work, it is necessary to begin with the first article and the concepts of classification and framing.

The concept of classification is at the heart of Bernstein's theory of curriculum. Classification refers to 'the degree of boundary maintenance between contents' (Bernstein 1973a: 205; 1973b: 88) and is concerned with the insulation or boundaries between curricular categories (areas of knowledge and subjects). Strong classification refers to a curriculum that is highly differentiated and separated into traditional subjects; weak classification refers to a curriculum that is integrated and in which the boundaries between subjects are fragile.

Using the concept of classification, Bernstein outlined two types of curriculum codes: collection and integrated codes. The first refers to a strongly classified curriculum; the latter, to a weakly classified curriculum. In keeping with his Durkheimian project, Bernstein analysed the way in which the shift from collection to integrated curriculum codes represents the evolution from mechanical to organic solidarity, with curricular change marking the movement from the sacred to the profane.

Whereas classification is concerned with the organization of knowledge into curriculum, framing is related to the transmission of knowledge through pedagogic practices. Framing refers to the location of control over the rules of communication and, according to Bernstein (1990c: 100) 'if classification regulates the voice of a category then framing regulates the form of its legitimate message.' Furthermore, 'frame refers to the degree of control teacher and pupil possess over the selection, organization, pacing and timing of the knowledge transmitted and received in the pedagogical relationship' (1973b: 88). Therefore, strong framing refers to a limited degree of options between teacher and students; weak framing implies more freedom.

In keeping with the Durkheimian project, Bernstein's inquiry into the organization (curriculum) and transmission of knowledge (pedagogy) sought to relate shifts in classification and framing to the evolution of the social division of labour. In 'Class and pedagogies: visible and invisible' (1977b), he demonstrated how the move to an integrated code with weak classification and weak framing represents conflicts between the positioning of the old and new middle classes in the social division of labour and provides an illuminating examination of how pedagogic discourse and practice are structurally related to shifts in social structure. Moreover, although Bernstein was not a Marxist, he incorporated class and power relations into an overall social theory, as he did in all his work.

15

Following this earlier work on curriculum and pedagogic practice was a detailed analysis of pedagogic discourse (1986, 1990a) that presented a highly complex analysis of the recontextualization of knowledge through the pedagogic device. As Atkinson noted:

> At the heart of the 'pedagogic device' is the coding of power whereby the 'thinkable' is discriminated and demarcated, in a fashion which corresponds to the function of 'classification.' In modern, complex societies the contrast between the 'sacred' and the 'profane' is formally paralleled by the classificatory principles emanating from the higher reaches of the education system. The pedagogic device is a mechanism for the distribution of the 'thinkable' among different social groups, for the identification of what may be thought simultaneously implies who may think it. Social order is thus equivalent to the cosmological order of legitimate categories of consciousness.
>
> (Atkinson 1985: 173)

Thus, Bernstein's work on pedagogic discourse was concerned with the production, distribution and reproduction of official knowledge and how this knowledge is related to structurally determined power relations. What is critical is that Bernstein was concerned with more than the description of the production and transmission of knowledge; he was concerned with its consequences for different groups. Whereas his work on pedagogic discourse was concerned more with the classification rules of the pedagogic device (that is, in the production and reproduction of knowledge) his work on pedagogic practice returned to framing rules and there he was directly interested in the transmission of knowledge. Once again, Bernstein returned to the manner in which social class and power relations affect pedagogic practice.

Bernstein's analysis of pedagogic practice begins with the distinction between a 'pedagogic practice as a cultural relay and a pedagogic practice in terms of what it relays' (1990b: 63). That is, Bernstein looked at the process and content of what occurs inside schools in terms of the 'how' and the 'what'. The theory of pedagogic practice examined a series of rules that define its inner logic and considers both how these rules affect the content to be transmitted and, perhaps more important, how they 'act selectively on those who can successfully acquire it' (1990b: 63).

From a detailed analysis of these rules, Bernstein examined 'the social class assumptions and consequences of forms of pedagogic practice' (1990b: 63). Finally, he applied this theory first to oppositional forms of pedagogic practice (conservative/traditional versus progressive/child-centred)' and, second, to oppositional types within the conservative/traditional form. He differentiated between a pedagogic practice that is dependent on the economic market – that emphasizes vocational education – and another that is independent and autonomous of the market – that is legitimated by the autonomy of knowledge. Through a detailed analysis of these two competing traditional ideological forms, Bernstein concluded that both forms, despite their claims to the contrary, will not eliminate the reproduction of class inequalities. Thus, through a careful and logical consideration of the inner workings of the dominant forms of educational practice, Bernstein contributed to a greater understanding of how schools (especially in the United States) reproduce what they are ideologically committed to eradicating – social-class advantages in schooling and society.

Bernstein's analysis of the social-class assumptions of pedagogic practice is the foundation for linking micro-educational processes to the macro-sociological levels of social structure and class and power relations. His basic thesis is that there are significant differences in the social-class assumptions of VPs and IPs and despite these differences between what he terms 'opposing modalities of control' (1990b: 73), there may indeed be similar outcomes, especially in the reproduction of power and symbolic control.

Much of the criticism of Bernstein's early work revolved around issues of deficit and difference. It is important to note here that Bernstein rejected the view that his work was based on either a deficit or a difference approach. Rather, he argued that his code theory attempted to connect the macro-levels of family and educational structures and processes and to provide an explanation for unequal educational performance. He stated:

> The code theory asserts that there is a social class regulated unequal distribution of privileging principles of communication ... and that social class, indirectly, affects the classification and framing of the elaborated code transmitted by the school so as to facilitate and perpetuate its unequal acquisition. Thus the code theory accepts neither a deficit nor a difference position but draws attention to the relations between macro power relations and micro practices of transmission, acquisition and evaluation and the positioning and oppositioning to which these practices give rise.
>
> (1990c: 118–119)

Thus, from his early work on code theory to the more recent works on pedagogic discourse (1986) and pedagogic practices (1990b), Bernstein's project sought to link microprocesses (language, transmission and pedagogy) to macroforms – to how cultural and educational codes and the content and process of education are related to social class and power relations.

Karabel and Halsey (1977: 71) stated that one of the most unresolved problems of Bernstein's work was how 'power relationships penetrate the organization, distribution and evaluation of knowledge through the social context' (Bernstein 1970: 347). Over the past 25 years, Bernstein continued to search for answers to this question and developed an increasingly sophisticated model for understanding how the classification and framing rules of the official pedagogic field affect the transmission, the distribution and, perhaps, the transformation of consciousness, and how these processes are indirectly related to the economic field of production. His positing of an indirect relation of education to production and his emphasis on the manner in which the realm of symbolic control does not directly correspond to the economic field did not answer his neo-Marxist critics. However, this work continued his attempt to demonstrate the interrelationships between the economy, the family and the school, and how educational practices reflect complex tensions in these relationships.

As a theoretical model, Bernstein's work presents, in painstaking detail, the rules of pedagogic discourse and practices and a comprehensive picture of both the 'what' (classification rules) and the 'how' (framing rules) of educational systems. Furthermore, his work on pedagogic practice (1990b) attempted to link these micro and institutional processes to educational change and opens an exciting but as yet undeveloped avenue of inquiry. Bernstein conceded that those who seek answers to difficult educational questions often prefer a top-down approach – one that begins with the large policy questions and builds down to an analysis of how the schools work to provide solutions or to constrain their formulation. He admitted, however, that the nature of his project was to build from the bottom to the top – an approach that seeks to write the rules of educational process; then to link them to larger structural conditions; and, finally, to place this analysis in the context of the larger educational and policy questions of educators (1990c).

Bernstein's project, then, from his early work on language, to the development of code theory, to the work on curriculum and pedagogic practice, was to develop a systematic theory that provides an analytic description of the way in which the educational system is related to the social division of labour. Because his work dealt with so many of the themes central to the development of sociological theory, he was often portrayed as a neo-Marxist, a functionalist, a Weberian conflict theorist, or an interactionist new sociologist of education. Code theory, taken as a whole, however, had at its core the goal of his entire project: to develop a Durkheimian theory that analyses the way in which changes in the division of labour create different meaning systems and codes, that provides analytic classifications of these systems, and that incorporates a conflict model of unequal power relations into its structural approach.

Atkinson (1981, 1985) argued that the evolution of Bernstein's sociology must be understood as the movement from its early Durkheimian roots to a later convergence with European structuralist thought, especially French social theory. In the United States, however, because the Durkheimian tradition was appropriated both by Parsonian structural functionalism and by positivism, Bernstein's work was, at times, incorrectly viewed as conservative. For example, Karabel and Halsey's (1977) treatment of Bernstein as the 'harbinger of a new synthesis' speaks of his need to link his Durkheimian perspective more explicitly to neo-Marxist categories. While his work on pedagogic practice clearly does link the two, Bernstein never moved out of a Durkheimian position; rather, he incorporated the neo-Marxist and Weberian categories of class and power relations into his overall theory. It is necessary to remove the consensus aspects of functionalism that are associated with structural functionalism to understand Bernstein's sociology. Although his work has been concerned with how communication, cultural and educational codes function in relation to particular social structures, Bernstein was concerned not with the way in which such functioning leads to consensus but with how it forms the basis of privilege and domination.

It is with respect to the relationship with privilege and domination that Bernstein's work, while remaining consistent with a Durkheimian foundation, systematically integrated Marxism and Weberian categories and provided the possibilities for the synthesis that Karabel and Halsey called for. Bernstein's work continued to be Durkheimian because, as Atkinson (1985: 36) pointed out, an essential activity has been the exploration of changes from mechanical to organic solidarity through an analysis of the division of labour, boundary maintenance, social roles, the ritual-expressive order, cultural categories, social control and types of messages. It attempted to look at modes of cultural transmission through the analysis of codes. In addition, his work continued to link classification and framing codes to the unequal distribution of resources in capitalist societies. While the original article on class and pedagogy was clearly more Durkheimian in its analysis of changes in organic solidarity, his later work (Bernstein 1990b, 1996) was more interested in the consequences of different pedagogic practices for different social classes and, most important, returns to the very questions of education and inequality that were the original basis of the project over 30 years ago.

Thus, Bernstein's work on pedagogic discourses and practice accomplishes a number of related and important things. First, it provided a theory of school knowledge and transmission and demonstrates how the what of education is transmitted. Second, it linked the sociolinguistic aspects of his early work to the analysis of the codes of schooling. Third, in relating the process and content of transmission to differences in social class and in calling for an analysis of the consequences of those differences in curriculum and pedagogy, Bernstein provided a tentative integration of structuralist and conflict approaches within sociology. Most theories of cultural reproduction (Bourdieu 1973; Bourdieu and Passeron 1977; Giroux 1981, 1983), according to Bernstein, are theories of distorted communication without theories of communication; they are not 'concerned with descriptions of the carrier, only with a diagnosis of its pathology' (Bernstein 1996: 10); and they 'are incapable of generating specific descriptions of the agencies relevant to their concerns' (9).

Over the last three decades, Bernstein's work has been the subject of considerable criticism and controversy. Bernstein (1990c) classified a typology of different types of criticism and argues that much of his work has been taken out of context or recontextualized incorrectly. Much of the criticism has not been based on a close reading of his work, but rather on secondary interpretations. The major criticism of his early sociolinguistic work as 'cultural deficit' theory has diverted attention from his larger body of work. Thus, Danzig (1995) correctly points out, Bernstein is often viewed narrowly in the context of sociolinguistics. The important point is that the early work on social class and language was part of a larger, ongoing sociological project. From the outset, Bernstein was concerned with connecting the levels of sociological analysis: societal, institutional, interactional and intrapsychic (see Persell 1977) and understanding the ways in which meanings are transmitted to individuals, from the division of labour, through the family and the schools. Code theory is then an overarching sociological approach to understanding how consciousness is dialectically related to the division of labour, especially in terms of differences between the fields of production (economic), symbolic control (culture) and institutions (family and school), and how meaning systems are relayed, transmitted and acquired. Most importantly, Bernstein's sociology places power squarely in the equation. Although the emphasis of Bernstein's work, especially since the 1970s, has been on schooling, his project has always proceeded from a theoretical base. His theoretical approach has been labelled Durkheimian, neo-Marxist, structuralist and interactionist, as well as being part of the 'new sociology'. Bernstein (1996) stated that these have been the labels of others and that they have often been too exclusive, often simplifying the theoretical complexity of his model. He acknowledged that Durkheim has always been at the heart of his sociological theory: in part as a corrective to the conservative interpretation of Durkheim's work, especially in the United States; in part as a consequence of Parson's structural-functional interpretation of Durkheim. Additionally, although he acknowledged the structuralist interpretations of his work by Atkinson (1985) and Sadovnik (1991), he did not see his work as exclusively structuralist. He rejected the view that he was part of the 'new sociology', as he believed that his work was 'old' sociology, particularly in terms of its roots in classical sociological theory. Finally, he suggested that the idea that it was his project to connect disparate sociological theories was not his but was suggested by others, particularly Karabel and Halsey (1977). Although their labelling of his work as the 'harbinger of a new synthesis' was complimentary, it also raised an expectation of a kind of synthesis that has not been explicitly part of his project. Rather than working from one sociological theory, or attempting to synthesize a number of theories, Bernstein attempted to develop and refine a model that is capable of describing the complex interrelationships between different aspects of society.

Whatever the criticisms of his work, it is undeniable that Bernstein's work represents one of the most sustained and powerful attempts to investigate significant issues in the sociology of education. Forty years ago, Bernstein began with a simple but overwhelming issue: how to find ways to 'prevent the wastage of working-class educational potential' (1961: 308). The problem of educability led to the development of code theory. Code theory, while a powerful and controversial perspective on educational inequality, did not sufficiently provide an understanding of what goes on inside the schools and how these practices are systematically related to social-class advantages and disadvantages. In an attempt to connect the macro and the micro further, Bernstein's work since the 1960s centred on a model of discourse and pedagogic practices, beginning with the concepts of classification and framing and continuing to a more systematic outline of the 'what' and the 'how' of education. Taken as a whole, Bernstein's work provided a systematic analysis of codes, pedagogic discourse and practice and their relationship to symbolic control and identity.

Basil Bernstein: mentor and friend

I first met Basil Bernstein in 1978 at New York University, when I was a doctoral student and he was a Visiting Professor. He took an interest in a paper I wrote for him applying his work to Bowles and Gintis's *Schooling in Capitalist America* (1976). For the next 22 years, he was my mentor, colleague and, most of all, beloved friend. His impact on my career (as well as dozens of his other students now in prestigious university positions all over the world) was enormous. Upon telling him that I received the American Sociological Association's Willard Waller Award for my article on his work, he replied with his usual sense of humour: 'My dear boy, I *have* made your career, haven't I?'

As a mentor, he was giving of his time and support. Although he responded favourably to my work on his work, he nonetheless responded with long letters, always handwritten, always difficult to decipher, pointing to things I had overlooked, new ways of seeing, and full of new insights. While some warned that writing about his work could damage our friendship, it never did. Even when he disagreed with my interpretations, he never asked that I change a word. The process of editing *Knowledge and Pedagogy* was one of the most intense and satisfying experiences of my career. Basil read and wrote responses to many of the articles in the book; his correspondence on the book is filled with incredible contributions to my own thinking, only a portion of it included in his epilogue. Most of all, Basil never forgot that it was my book, not his, and after providing feedback, left the final editing to me. For the next 22 years, what began with me watching his incredible mind work out models from CCC Volume 3 at NYU, continued as I moved from doctoral student to professor: Basil helped me to understand the complexities of schooling and social reproduction. As a teacher, he inspired me to help my own students grow and develop intellectually; as a scholar, he inspired me to think sociologically and to insist upon empirical research to support theory. That I have attained some reputation as an expert on his work is testimony to his success as a mentor.

What I will always cherish is his friendship. What I remember most are the wonderful times we had with Basil and his wife Marion at their lovely home in Dulwich, at the National Theatre, at the Tate Gallery, shopping at Harvey Nichols, Liberty's and in Bond Street, and eating and drinking in numerous restaurants near the Institute in Bloomsbury. Professor Bernstein was no narrow academic. He was an arts aficionado, most proud of his David Hockneys; an audiophile, who moved reluctantly from his precious LP collection to CDs; an expert photographer, who was as proud of his photo of Susan Semel in the Hofstra University Research Magazine, complete with the credit, 'photograph by Basil Bernstein', as he was of a journal article; a beau brummel, fond of Armani and Kenzo. He is the only academic who could tell me precisely where on Bond Street Gucci and Zegna were located; and he was the only academic I know to be on a first name basis with the maitre d's at Liberty's Restaurant and the Fifth Floor Restaurant at Harvey Nichols. Oh, how he loved the Oyster Bar at Bibendum and a fine Chianti Classico! And what a conversationalist he was: ironic, creative, clever, amusing, knowledgeable and, at times, cryptic and sardonic. Whether it was applying code theory to the exploitation of South American farmers at one of his favourite

Bloomsbury haunts, Isolabella, or, with Eliot Freidson, entertaining us with their tales of 1968 at Berkeley, Basil was one of a kind.

When I first met Basil in 1978, I told him that I had grown up in Far Rockaway, a New York City beach community and that I had been a surfer and skateboarder. He asked me to go to the Rockaway Beach Surf Shop and buy him a real California skateboard to take home to his young son Francis, who he said loved skateboarding. His dedication to the fifth volume of *Class, Codes and Control* in 1996, as of the first in 1971, reads simply 'For Marion', summing up the incredible devotion they had for each other, a partnership in every sense of the word.

The last time I saw Basil was in June 2000 after a conference in Lisbon, organized by Ana Morais, Isabel Neves, Harry Daniels and Brian Davies, on his contributions to educational research. Too ill to attend as planned, Basil participated on Friday for the last hour via video link to his home in London. Despite being weak from treatment, he was vintage Basil: witty, creative, and dressed for the occasion in one of his favourite silk shirts. His brief written contribution on code theory and technology provided significant food for thought. Upon termination of the link, there was not a dry eye among us. We all knew that this might have been his last public appearance and we all knew how much we would miss him.

On the Sunday following the conference, Susan Semel and I visited Basil and Marion in London. Although weak, he spoke of finishing CCC, Volume 6, of applying code theory to the internet and technology, and of New Labour's educational policy – still, in his view, like that of Thatcher's, 'a new pedagogical janus...'(1990) reproducing the old inequalities. Although I left hoping it was not a final goodbye, I knew that it might well be. And it was. When Basil Bernstein died on 24 September 2000 the world of sociology lost a giant. I lost a mentor and friend to whom I will always be grateful.

References

Atkinson, P. (1981) 'Bernstein's structuralism', *Educational Analysis* 3: 85–96.

Atkinson, P. (1985) *Language, Structure and Reproduction: An introduction to the sociology of Basil Bernstein*. London: Methuen.

Atkinson, P., Davies, B., and Delamont, S. (1995) *Discourse and Reproduction: Essays in honor of Basil Bernstein*. Cresskill, NJ: Hampton Press.

Bernstein, B. (1958) 'Some sociological determinants of perception: an enquiry into sub-cultural differences', *British Journal of Sociology* 9: 159–74.

Bernstein, B. (1960) 'Language and social class: a research note', *British Journal of Sociology* 11: 271–6.

Bernstein, B. (1961a) 'Social class and linguistic development: a theory of social learning', in A.H. Halsey, J. Floud and C.A. Anderson (eds) *Education, Economy and Society*. New York: Free Press: 288–314.

Bernstein, B. (1961b) 'Social structure, language, and learning', *Educational Research* 3: 163–76.

Bernstein, B. (1962a)'Linguistic codes, hesitation phenomena and intelligence', *Language and Speech* 5: 31–46.

Bernstein, B. (1962b) 'Social class, linguistic codes and grammatical elements', *Language and Speech* 5: 221–40.

Bernstein, B. (1970) 'Education cannot compensate for society', *New Society*, 387: 344–7.

Bernstein, B. (1973a) *Class, Codes and Control: Vol. 1*. London: Routledge and Kegan Paul. (Originally published in 1971.)

Bernstein, B. (1973b) 'On the classification and framing of educational knowledge', in B. Bernstein, *Class, Codes and Control: Vol. 1* (pp. 202–30) and *Class, Codes and Control: Vol. 2* (pp. 85–115). London: Routledge and Kegan Paul. (Originally published in M.F.D. Young (ed.) *Knowledge and Control: New directions for the sociology of education*. London: Collier-Macmillan, 1971.)

Bernstein, B. (1973c) *Class, Codes and Control: Vol. 2*. London: Routledge and Kegan Paul. (Originally published in 1971.)

Bernstein, B. (1977a) *Class, Codes and Control: Vol. 3*. London: Routledge and Kegan Paul. (Originally published in 1975.)

Bernstein, B. (1977b) 'Class and pedagogies: visible and invisible' (rev. edn), in B. Bernstein, *Class, Codes and Control: Vol. 3*. London: Routledge and Kegan Paul: 116–56).

Bernstein, B. (1986) 'On pedagogic discourse', in J.G. Richardson (ed.) *Handbook for Theory and Research in the Sociology of Education*. New York: Greenwood: 205–40. (Revised and reprinted in Bernstein 1990d: 165–218.)

Bernstein, B. (1990a) *Class, Codes and Control: Vol. 4: The Structuring of Pedagogic Discourse*. London: Routledge.

Bernstein, B. (1990b) 'Social class and pedagogic practice', in B. Bernstein, *Class, Codes and Control: Vol. 4. The Structuring of Pedagogic Discourse*. London: Routledge: 63–93.

Bernstein, B. (1990c) 'Elaborated and restricted codes: overview and criticisms', in B. Bernstein, *Class, Codes and Control: Vol. 4: The Structuring of Pedagogic Discourse*. London: Routledge: 94–130.

Bernstein, B. (1990d) 'The social construction of pedagogic discourse', in B. Bernstein, *Class, Codes and Control: Vol. 4: The Structuring of Pedagogic Discourse*. London: Routledge: 165–218 .

Bernstein, B. (1996) *Pedagogy, Symbolic Control and Identity: Theory, research, critique*. London: Taylor and Francis.

Bourdieu, P. (1973) 'Cultural reproduction and social reproduction', in R. Brown (ed.) *Knowledge, Education, and Cultural Change*. London: Tavistock: 71–112.

Bourdieu, P. and Passeron, J.C. (1977) *Reproduction in Education, Society and Culture*. London: Sage.

Bowles, S. and Gintis, H. (1976) *Schooling in Capitalist America*. New York: Basic Books.

Danzig, A. (1995) 'Applications and distortions of Basil Bernstein's code theory', in A.R. Sadovnik (ed.) *Knowledge and Pedagogy: The sociology of Basil Bernstein*. Norwood, NJ: Ablex Publishing Corporation: 145–70.

Giroux, H. (1981) *Ideology, Culture and the Process of Schooling*. Philadelphia: Temple University Press.

Giroux, H. (1983) *Theory and Resistance in Education*. South Hadley, MA: Bergin and Garvey.

Karabel, J. and Halsey, A.H. (1977) *Power and Ideology in Education*. New York: Oxford University Press.

Persell, C.H. (1977) *Education and Inequality*. New York: Free Press.

Sadovnik, A.R. (1991) 'Basil Bernstein's theory of pedagogic practice: a structuralist approach', *Sociology of Education* 64(1): 48–63.

Sadovnik, A.R. (ed.) (1995) *Knowledge and Pedagogy: The sociology of Basil Bernstein*. Norwood, NJ: Ablex Publishing Corporation.

Young, M.F.D. (ed.) (1971) *Knowledge and Control: New directions for the sociology of education*. London: Collier-Macmillan.

A RECITAL OF SONGS
AND POEMS

Peter Hayward (counter-tenor)
Yu-Ching Cheng (piano)
Stavria Kotsoni-Brown (cello)
Professor Julia Brannen (reader)

'Dove sei'
Music by George Frederick Handel
From *Rodelinda*

Dove sei, amato bene?
Vieni l'alma a consolar!
Vieni, vieni, amato bene!
Son oppresso da tormenti,
Ed I crudi miei lamenti
Sol con te posso bear.

(Where are you, beloved?
Come to soothe my soul!
Come beloved!
I am tormented
And only with you
Can I bear my sadness.)

'Esurientes'
Music by Johann Sebastian Bach
From the *Magnificat*

Esurientes, implevit bonus et divites dimisit inanes.
(He hath filled the hungry with good things and the rich he
hath sent empty away.)

'An Evening Hymn'
Music by Henry Purcell
Words by 'Dr William Fuller, late Lord-Bishop of Lincoln'

Now, now that the sun hath veiled his light and bid the world good night;
To the soft bed my body I dispose,
But where shall be soul repose?
Dear God, even in thy arms,
And can there be any so sweet security!
Then to thy rest, Oh my soul!
And singing, praise the mercy that prolongs thy days.
Hallelujah!

Psalm 113

Praise ye the Lord. Praise, O ye servants of the Lord, praise the name of the
  Lord.
Blessed be the name of the Lord from this time forth and for evermore.
From the rising of the sun unto the going down of the same the Lord's
  name is to be praised.
The Lord is high above all nations, and his glory above the heavens.
Who is like unto the Lord our God, that hath his seat on high,
That humbleth himself to behold the things that are in heaven and in the
  earth?
He raiseth up the poor out of the dust, and lifteth up the needy out of the
  dunghill;
That he may set him with princes, even with the princes of his people.
He maketh the barren women to keep house, and to be a joyful mother of
  children. Praise ye the Lord.

From 'The Ninth Elegy'
Rainer Maria Rilke, translated by J.B. Leishman

Why, when this span of life might be fleeted away
as laurel, a little darker than all
the surrounding green, with tiny waves on the border
of every leaf (like the smile of a wind):– oh, why
have to be human, and, shunning Destiny,
long for Destiny?...

                    Not because happiness really
exists, that precipitate profit of imminent loss.
Not out of curiosity, not just to practise the heart,
that could still be there in laurel....
But because being here is much, and because all this
that's here, so fleeting, seems to require us and strangely
concerns us. Us the most fleeting of all. Just once,
everything, only for once. Once and no more. And we, too,
once. And never again. But this
having been once, though only once,
having been once on earth – can it ever be cancelled?

'Aubade'
Philip Larkin

I work all day, and get half-drunk at night.
Waking at four to soundless dark, I stare.
In time the curtain-edges will grow light.
Till then I see what's really always there:
Unresting death, a whole day nearer now,
Making all thought impossible but how
And where and when I shall myself die.
Arid interrogation: yet the dread
Of dying, and being dead,
Flashes afresh to hold and horrify.

The mind blanks at the glare. Not in remorse
– The good not done, the love not given, time
Torn off unused – nor wretchedly because
An only life can take so long to climb
Clear of its wrong beginnings, and may never;
But at the total emptiness for ever,
The sure extinction that we travel to
And shall be lost in always. Not to be here,
Not be anywhere,
And soon; nothing more terrible, nothing more true.

This is a special way of being afraid
No trick dispels. Religion used to try,
That vast moth-eaten musical brocade
Created to pretend we never die,
And specious stuff that says *No rational being*
Can fear a thing it will not feel, not seeing
That this is what we fear – no sight, no sound,
No touch or taste or smell, nothing to think with,
Nothing to love or link with,
The anaesthetic from which none come round.

And so it stays just on the edge of vision,
A small unfocused blur, a standing chill
That slows each impulse down to indecision.
Most things may never happen: this one will,
And realisation of it rages out
In furnace-fear when we are caught without
People or drink. Courage is no good:
It means not scaring others. Being brave
Lets no one off the grave.
Death is no different whined at than withstood.

Slowly light strengthens, and the room takes shape.
It stands plain as a wardrobe, what we know,
Have always known, know that we can't escape,
Yet can't accept. One side will have to go.
Meanwhile telephones crouch, getting ready to ring
In locked-up offices, and all the uncaring
Intricate rented world begins to rouse.
The sky is white as clay, with no sun.
Work has to be done.
Postmen like doctors go from house to house.

'Mending wall'
Robert Frost

Something there is that doesn't love a wall,
That sends the frozen-ground-swell under it
And spills the upper boulders in the sun,
And makes gaps even two can pass abreast.
The work of hunters is another thing:
I have come after them and made repair
Where they have left not one stone on a stone,
But they would have the rabbit out of hiding,
To please the yelping dogs. The gaps I mean,
No one has seen them made or heard them made,
But at spring mending-time we find them there.
I let my neighbor know beyond the hill;
And on a day we meet to walk the line
And set the wall between us once again.
We keep the wall between us as we go.
To each the boulders that have fallen to each.
And some are loaves and some so nearly balls
We have to use a spell to make them balance:
'Stay where you are until our backs are turned!'
We wear our fingers rough with handling them.
Oh, just another kind of outdoor game,
One on a side. It comes to little more:
There where it is we do not need the wall:
He is all pine and I am apple orchard.
My apple trees will never get across

And eat the cones under his pines, I tell him.
He only says, 'Good fences make good neighbors.'
Spring is the mischief in me, and I wonder
If I could put a notion in his head:
'*Why* do they make good neighbors? Isn't it
Where there are cows? But here there are no cows.
Before I built a wall I'd ask to know
What I was walling in or walling out,
And to whom I was like to give offense.
Something there is that doesn't love a wall,
That wants it down.' I could say 'Elves' to him,
But it's not elves exactly, and I'd rather
He said it for himself. I see him there,
Bringing a stone grasped firmly by the top
In each hand, like an old-stone savage armed.
He moves in darkness as it seems to me,
Not of woods only and the shade of trees.
He will not go behind his father's saying,
And he likes having thought of it so well
He says again, 'Good fences make good neighbors.'

'Untitled'
Basil Bernstein

There is no way of knowing how it is
Until it's too late to show
There is no way of showing how it is
Until it's too late to care
There is no way of saying how it is
Until it's too late to share
There is no way of feeling how it is
Until it's too late to know

CROSSING BOUNDARIES BETWEEN DISCIPLINES

A perspective on Basil Bernstein's legacy

Ana Maria Morais, Professor of Education,
University of Lisbon, Portugal

'YOU MAY STAY IF you wish but I don't think this is going to be of much use to you.' That's how I was allowed into Professor Bernstein's seminars some twenty years ago.

I am not a sociologist. I am a science educator. At that time science education was again in a consensual state of crisis. After the international enthusiasm of the new science education of the 1960s and 1970s, it was evident that students were not achieving the level of scientific literacy that was expected of them. New lines of research were developing based on psychology and epistemology, that is, within the same paradigm as previous science education developments. Everything I had been doing at that time in teacher training, curriculum development and classroom teaching was also founded on those same kinds of assumption. Arriving in London at this Institute I was feeling that I was having more of the same. By chance, I came across a paper by Basil Bernstein and immediately felt I wanted to attend his seminars.

The first time I went there I clearly saw two apparently contradictory things. First I didn't understand most of what he was saying. Second, what he was saying was definitely what I wanted to learn.

In time, Professor Bernstein agreed to supervise my PhD thesis. And in time Professor Bernstein became Basil.

That's how everything started. Later on, back home I managed to pass on my interests to others and, with the invaluable help of my research students and of my students' research students, we initiated a line of research which departed from all science education research done at the time.

Science educators have always resisted the sociological. Apart from some theoretically poorly grounded research on gender and vague cultural issues, their interests did not go much further. Only recently, in the 1990s, have a few turned to Vygotsky as a way of considering the social context of the science classroom. The general rejection by science educators of sociological approaches is very deep and can be seen as having many roots. I am just going to refer here to one of them.

Experimental sciences are vertical structures of knowledge. Theories of instruction are horizontal structures of knowledge. That is to say the *what* to be taught in science classes is quite distinct in its structure from the *how* to be taught. Science educators have been primarily socialized within specific vertical structures of knowledge and they have always found some difficulty in accepting knowledges characterized by parallel languages.

However, because of the strong grammar that characterizes psychology, science educators have accepted more willingly its knowledges as a grounding for science education than they have accepted the knowledges of sociology, characterized by weak grammars. In general, they tend to feel that sociology is very 'loose', poorly conceptualized and unable to help them with their research and practice.

In my view, this constitutes a serious problem for improving science education because sociological analysis is then in general discarded as non-relevant. However, Basil Bernstein's theory constitutes a remarkable exception. I contend that Bernstein's theory, which departs from other sociological theories in many aspects, can be seen as characterized by a strong grammar because 'it has an explicit conceptual syntax capable of "relatively" precise empirical descriptions and/or of generating formal modelling of empirical relations' (Bernstein 1999). And this may be one of the many reasons why some science educators have been more willing to accept it. In fact, the strong conceptualization that it contains, its evolution to higher and higher levels of abstraction, its power of description, explanation, diagnosis, prediction and transferability have appealed to science educators. These science educators are those who have an interest in the sociological (including the Vygotskian followers, but not only them) and who have found in Bernstein's theory a 'form of thinking' closer to the vertical structures in which they were socialized.

However, many have felt that the theory is very complex and have not been prepared to make the effort to learn it. They have already been socialized into psychological and epistemological theories and most sociological analyses and interventions have led them to think it is not worth the effort. And, because they don't know the theory, they have not been aware of how much they are missing in their educational analysis and intervention.

If things are somewhat different in my own country, it is because my former science education students and myself have systematically taught Bernstein's theory and the empirical research based on it to undergraduate and research students. This has always been done not by undervaluing psychological and epistemological approaches but by giving to sociological approaches the same level of importance. In this way we have tried to weaken the classification between usually strongly classified fields, that is, we have pushed further something Basil Bernstein did himself.

In fact, without losing his identity as a great sociologist, Bernstein has always made links with other areas of knowledge such as psychology, linguistics, anthropology and epistemology. My contention is that this is but one of the many reasons why his theory has been widely used across different areas of knowledge. But it is also one of the reasons why many sociologists have not accepted it easily and have criticized it for so long. Their identities have been formed in the strongly classified knowledge of sociology and its weak grammar and they reject any attempt at blurring the boundaries between disciplines. Many think that Bernstein's work stopped thirty years ago and hence their critique is only directed at his former work. But I believe that what lies behind this is much related to the fact that his theory departs from other sociological theories in many crucial aspects. Bernstein's theory has a very strong conceptual structure which places it, as I said before, within the horizontal structures of knowledge of strong grammars and even, I would say, in many aspects, within a vertical structure of knowledge.

The way Bernstein has developed his theory can be seen as having features of the way theories in experimental sciences have developed. It is extremely interesting to think of it as within a rationalist view, where a model is first constructed and a methodological approach is defined to open the way for the work of researchers, to its testing, modification and enlargement. And this is again another feature which is not easily accepted by many sociologists. The power of description, explanation, diagnosis, prediction, transferability, which is part of the greatness of Bernstein's theory, is again a reason for rejection of something many sociologists do not share.

So far I have not used the word ideology, but that is what I have been talking about when looking at the positioning towards Bernstein's theory of science educators on the one hand and of sociologists on the other. Surely, what I have said is just a very restricted perspective on Bernstein's legacy.

Coming back to science education, I believe that I have brought into it a new dimension, in both research and educational practices. But I also know that this has hardly yet passed beyond my own country. And this, again, is sociological. Were I British or American, things might be different. I do hope that, in the future, science educators can see the gains for their research and practices if Bernstein's views are *really* included in science education.

As for me, I must say that to have done a PhD thesis under his supervision was a difficult experience but one I shall never forget. Just as I shall never forget the discussions and support I always found in the work following the thesis. That is why in my thesis I acknowledged him for his willingness to overcome difficulties in crossing boundaries of established disciplines and conceptual frameworks.

But I owe him much more than that. He changed my whole mind, my whole way of looking at the world ... and he was also a very great friend.

That is why I am so very honoured and yet saddened, too, to be here today.

Reference
Bernstein, B. (1999) 'Vertical and horizontal discourse: an essay', *British Journal of Sociology of Education* 20(2): 157–74.

THE LEGACY OF BASIL BERNSTEIN

Paul Atkinson, Cardiff School of Social Sciences,
Cardiff University

IT IS OF COURSE right to think of Basil's legacy for future sociologists when – understandably – the tendency is to look back in reviewing and celebrating his life and his work. But to look ahead and to speculate on Basil's future influence is not easy. Of course, only time will tell. For sociology is an especially difficult subject to think about in these terms. Its collective attitude to its own protagonists is a peculiar one. Collectively sociologists seem to have two main attitudes towards their mentors and their progenitors. They swither between reverence and amnesia. When they are reverent, they canonize intellectual heroes – very rarely heroines. They position themselves as interpreters, hagiographers and disciples. They revere key works as sacred texts and devote themselves to their scriptural exegesis, quoting authority rather than devoting themselves to original thought of their own. Or – and this seems to happen a very great deal – they engage in a variety of collective amnesia. Major bodies of scholarship are neglected. Sociologists chase the ball all over the park, always in search of something new. If the novelty happens to derive from France or Germany, then so much the better. They search for the novel and the exotic. In the process our own British sociologists are too easily overlooked. Moreover, the rush for novel theories runs faster than the hard and more laborious work of sustained research programmes.

Whatever the future holds, therefore, we should not want either of those fates to overtake Basil and his work. He should not be treated as a figure to be frozen in time. He deserves better than to be preserved in aspic. Moreover, his ideas have always been intended to drive a programme of original inquiry: neither he nor we will benefit from their transformation into a body of sacred texts. His work will not be well served if it is turned into an arcane specialism of textual interpretation. Goodness only knows that there is ample opportunity for that: the texts have never been transparently accessible. But neither his memory nor his legacy will be well served by the creation of a cottage industry of Bernstein experts. Still less will his work be served by their incorporation into the simplicities of textbook sociology – a fate that all too commonly awaits the revered sociological theorist. Too many of today's – and no doubt tomorrow's – sociologists are in pursuit of sound-bite summaries and slogans. Bernstein's sociology did not readily lend itself to simple summary. When it was so summarized then it was all too often travestied and vulgarized, as we know.

But more than anything else, Basil does not merit the fate of sociological amnesia. Collectively, we have a dreadful capacity to forget the work of others and of forebears. In the absence of collective memory, sociology repeatedly reinvents the wheel. Many of the current claims of contemporary sociology – often under the influence of theoretical enthusiasm – appear to be novel only because too many people are ignorant of past achievements. Current sociology recapitulates the past under the guise of the new. Obviously Basil deserves more and better than to be the victim of sociological amnesia. Not least when social scientists re-discover the themes of language and identity; the cultural frameworks of knowledge and aesthetics; or the narratives of collective identity.

Hagiography, simplification, amnesia. Are these the only fates available for the sociologist and his work? I hope not. But I know that they are processes that Basil himself would have analysed with great panache. He analysed the circulation of texts, and the transformations that texts undergo as they migrate from one knowledge domain to another. He understood how ideas – his own included – become translated into the categories of pedagogic knowledge; how academic disciplines are defined by their own collective narratives of the past. And how disciplines define themselves as much by what they forget as by what they remember. We define what is known and what is thinkable by what we relegate to the margins and beyond them.

In that sense, then, Basil knew what to make of the very notion of a 'legacy'. For the notion of a legacy already projects a certain kind of future: a future that looks back. A discipline that defines itself in terms of forebears and culture-heroes. A patrimony of knowledge that is transmitted from generation to generation and is revered symbolically as one of the defining elements of the discipline. The academic discipline itself thus become self-defining – it recapitulates its so-called legacy by parcelling it up and passing it on deferentially from generation to generation. Academic enculturation into a discipline that deals mainly in 'legacies' will risk becoming a work of frozen texts that are progressively disengaged from the world about which it professes to speak. Ironically, sociology constantly risks that collapse into self-referential discourse. Basil deserves better. So if his work is a legacy, let it not be treated as an heirloom. Let it be a patrimony that is used and invested, and is itself transformed in the process.

Let Basil also be an example in himself. Sociologists are very ambivalent about role-models or heroes and – as I have said – he should not become an author whose works are studied for their own sake. But he does, through his work and through his life, provide us with important object lessons. He was his own man. He was well read and drew inspiration from some of the classic sociologists, anthropologists and linguists. But he never subsumed his own intellectual identity into that of others. His work stands as an example of someone who sustained a genuinely original train of thought over an entire career. Not without change and development. On the contrary, he was constantly reworking and refining the ideas, and repeatedly finding new ways to re-engage with his core preoccupations. As befitted the holder of the Karl Mannheim chair he was an independent and original intellectual. As befitted someone with his academic commitments, he achieved for himself a unique intellectual biography that stood apart from the vagaries of fashion. He also turned his own biography into an intellectual project. In doing so he under-stood and demonstrated that the biographical transcends the purely personal, and that narrative is more than mere story-telling.

He engaged with the themes of education – knowledge and ideology, curriculum and pedagogy, the fate of ideas – in a thoroughly serious way. He was critical – perhaps sometimes too critical – of much of the sociological work around him. He felt that others did not always grapple with the funda-mental issues. He never shrank from being a difficult thinker. His ideas do not translate easily into simple formulae. They demand serious attention. They reward the hard work that they require. For Basil consistently addressed the social and cultural transformations that are played out in the symbolic and organizational domains of education. He constantly reaffirmed that in educa-tional domains we witness struggle between competing world views. The educational field is not, he repeatedly affirmed, just an inert terrain on which are played out other social dramas. It is itself formed and transformed through cosmological and ideological contestation. The forms of education were his subject-matter – and they continue to furnish the subject-matter of sociolog-ical and anthropological analysis: the translation of ideas into commodities; of intellectual fields into markets; of professional craft into accreditation; of embodied knowledge into measurable outcomes. These remain a continuing research agenda central to the sociological imagination.

There is, too, an imperative to take on board a serious and systematic sociology of knowledge and pedagogy when our contemporary society is suffused with the didactic imperative. Beyond the narrowly defined boundaries of education, we are surrounded by presentations, narratives and exemplars. They define the narratives of the past through displays and spectacles of heritage – of nationhood and regional identity; of collective guilt and memory; of technological and aesthetic celebration. The everyday world is permeated and colonized by pedagogy: exhortations to moral, financial and physical self-improvement; documentary reportage and realism; the translation of the avant-garde into mass culture. These phenomena and others like them provide a contemporary agenda in which the sociology of education joins forces with other currents in sociology and other cultural disciplines. With such agendas and with the kinds of analytic insight that Basil provides, the sociology of education can place itself alongside the most influential of today's and tomorrow's intellectual developments.

In an age that celebrates reflexivity, Basil also gave us ways of under-standing our own cosmology in the academy. He gives us the intellectual tools to understand the profound changes that have overtaken the academy over the past decades. All of us in the United Kingdom experience them as the banal and intrusive hurts of successive exercises and reviews: of teaching quality and research output; of research training; of activity costing and so-called transparency. He helps us to understand the more profound symbolic systems that sustain and justify those impositions: the desire by the State and its agencies to transform the implicit into the explicit, to complete the work of modernity through the disenchantment of the academy; to undermine the trust that is the pre-contractual foundation of the social contract. He can help us to grasp and to resist the ideological processes that threaten to turn education into a series of total institutions; to reflect back the panopticist gaze that seeks to regulate our own intellectual work.

One of the intriguing features of the academy and its anthropology is the phenomenon of generations and lineages. As we get older the generations collapse. Students become colleagues before they become successors. I never was a student of Basil's – although I nearly became one, perhaps – but I first met him when I was a research student and he was already a well known and distinguished academic. As the years passed, and in response to his generosity, I took great pleasure from the fact that I was able to become, if not his intel-lectual equal, then at least a colleague in a relationship of mutual warmth and respect. It is now a privilege to be here today to reaffirm with you the enduring significance of his work and his personal influence for his contem-poraries, his students and his successors in sociology and beyond.

LUNCH-TIME TOAST

*Professor Sir William Taylor CBE, Director of the
Institute of Education 1973–1983*

Ladies and Gentlemen

I was privileged to know Basil for a little under half a century. Of all the many memories of those years, and of discussions with Basil as colleague, as critic, and even at one stage of our careers, as competitor, there is one type of encounter that stands out.

No, not in the Academic Board, or the Committee of Professors, or in his room in Gordon Square, but in the street.

Well before I returned to the Institute in 1973, and for many years after that, I used to run into Basil in those nearby streets and squares immortalised by members of the Bloomsbury Group. We might only speak for a few minutes. But in that time I would invariably learn something – about a conference I should take the trouble to attend, a journal article I should read, the work of a person whose work I hadn't heard of but which would repay attention, the high quality (or otherwise, for Basil did not readily indulge the otherwise) of a new recording of something by Mozart or by Mahler about which hitherto I had known nothing.

I would go away from these brief encounters excited by a new idea, set on catching up with a publication I'd missed, sometimes chastened by my readiness to express an opinion about something I hadn't taken the trouble properly to understand, but invariably keener than before we met to enquire, to read, to confer. Many such occasions would be followed a few days later by a note, a reference or two, or an off-print from Basil.

Such encounters are of the essence of academic life. I know I was not the only one to benefit from them.

Inevitably, academic interaction with Basil was not always comfortable. But then the life of the mind, properly pursued, is not a comfortable life. Human knowledge is not always advanced by emphasising the feel-good factor. To pursue intellectual life with integrity and with hope of productive outcome demands challenge, disproof, argument, contestation, constructive criticism. Basil offered these in plenty.

He eschewed the quicker satisfactions of the applied and the practical – although we need to remember that the theory of pedagogy was one of his central interests and, later on, for six years he proved an effective Pro-Director of this Institute, even, I believe, coming to enjoy aspects of administrative practice.

He continued, throughout his life, that struggle to make a real and permanent contribution to our deep understanding of how human beings interact with each other, in society generally and in education in particular, a struggle that is at the heart of what higher education in the University is about.

We salute his memory.

ON FIRST READING ...

Stephen J. Ball, Karl Mannheim Chair in the Sociology of Education, Institute of Education, University of London

I FIRST READ Basil Bernstein in 1971, 'On the classification and framing of educational knowledge'. It was a startling and bewildering experience. Here was a radically different and radically insightful way of analysing the hierarchies and divisions of the English education system. I have read the paper again many times since and each time things become clearer and new possibilities arise. The richness of the paper is still astonishing. This was one of three pieces of work that led me to want to become a sociologist of education, to do the sociology of education. I believe 'On the classification and framing ...' to be the best paper ever written in the sociology of education. I tried recently to convince Basil of this and to allow me to republish the paper in a collection I was editing. He was adamantly against my choice and suggested another much more recent paper and eventually I gave in to his preference. Although the paper he chose is excellent I regret now allowing him to convince me. If it is possible to not allow Basil to convince you. It is not just that the 1971 paper was important to me personally; it was also a milestone, a sort of coming of age paper in the sociology of education. It also set in train a process of theoretical development and elaboration that marks Basil out as the only general sociological theorist that British sociology of education has ever produced, although of course to all intents and purposes he was 'produced' elsewhere – in linguistics, anthropology and continental sociology. It is now difficult to read Bernstein and not see resonances with Bourdieu and Foucault but in 1971 those resonances were invisible to all but a few.

It is difficult to write about Basil in any kind of personal way without writing about yourself. The more I hear about Basil the more I realize that there were many Bernsteins. He related to and dealt with people very individually and very differently. I have no idea how to characterize my relationship with him. It sometimes seemed fragile but it survived, even if he once described me as the most discourteous book editor with whom he had ever dealt. I felt, although my work was very different in style and method from his own – he constantly berated me for failing to develop adequate 'languages of description' – that he respected me. He would often say to me 'you do the work'. I think I know but I wish now I had asked him exactly what he meant by that.

Our last meeting, shortly before his death, was extraordinary. I had expected the worst. I had been told how unwell he was. I know he was making a special effort, as he did for all his visitors, but our hour and a half was amazing. He was funny, cutting and stunningly sharp in equal measure. He ranged across a comparison of the impact of Durkheim and Weber on British sociology, a critique of cultural capital, and some new applications of the 'pedagogic device'. I struggled to get a word in. He also offered some advice about working at the Institute of Education which I shall endeavour to follow.

Conversations with Basil were always an adventure. You never knew where you would end up or what rocky shores might have to be navigated en route. But I shall miss the opportunity to listen to him and spar with him, travel in his company. I must read 'On the classification and framing ...' yet again.

THINKING ABOUT EDUCATION AND POWER IN KNOWLEDGE SOCIETIES

What are the implications of contemporary social change?

Lynne Chisholm, Visiting Professor in Education at the University of Newcastle and scientific advisor at the European Centre for the Development of Vocational Training in Thessaloniki, Greece

THE VERY PRELIMINARY THOUGHTS I want to present briefly today really began because I wrote something[1] of which Basil disapproved – at least initially. Many of us here will recall similar experiences – this is one of the things you could always count on, just as much as you could count on his genuine commitment to engaging with what he found interesting even, and perhaps especially, when he thought he might not like it.

It all comes down to the question of how to conceptualize and make sense of contemporary change, and most particularly how such change is expressed in the structures and processes of education in a broad sense of the term. None of the key theoretical analyses of the 1990s have systematically addressed this,[2] but have instead chosen to emphasize the economic, technological and broader cultural features of the transition to what, under a variety of designations, is generally understood to constitute a distinctive new social epoch, and which I have chosen to call that of knowledge societies.

For the last five years, I have worked in a European policymaking setting, that is, in a complex recontextualizing field, which negotiates, mediates and on occasion actively constructs official discourse on education, training and youth affairs. In comparison with the reach of national competence and influence on these matters, one could well argue that the European stage is relatively unimportant and ineffective. Yet broad trends of policy thinking across the European Union do find an expression in negotiations over what official Community discourse should and may promote with a view to supporting and complementing Member State policies and measures. The complexity of such negotiation processes, given their multilateral and inter-cultural character, is a fascinating subject for anyone's sociological imagination, but that is not on today's agenda.

As I moved into this setting in the mid-1990s, the notion of the knowledge society – originally *la société cognitive*, subsequently *la société de la connaissance*, and now overlain by the *knowledge-based economy* – had just definitively entered the education, training and youth arena.[3] In the meantime, the notion has firmly inserted itself as the prime reference point for positing the need for wide-ranging reform of institutionalized arrangements for teaching and learning throughout Europe. This, too, is a story worth telling. Unsurprisingly, however, the dominant motif expresses a concern to render education and training more responsive – to make systems and practices adapt, not change altogether – to the needs of changing labour markets, occupations and work processes. Most educationalists have an inherently allergic reaction to this kind of instrumental approach. I am no exception to that, and neither was Basil.

The more difficult consequential task is to marshal alternative approaches, at least those that might impact on the policy formulation process. But first we have to try to describe and understand what does or might happen to teaching and learning in knowledge societies, and in whose interests this could be. The production and reproduction of the social division of labour through pedagogic discourse as a crucial medium of symbolic control was the enduring focus of Basil's interest, and he concluded that understanding how this all works 'is probably more important today than at any other period.'[4]

The theory of pedagogic discourse may be attracting renewed attention precisely because it provides a starting point for describing and understanding the implications of contemporary change for the distribution of power and the shaping of consciousness through teaching and learning in all its forms.[5] And so, in an explicitly advertised trailer for the direction future work might take – and he already knew very well that it would not be his own work – he argued that we are witnessing, for the first time, 'a virtually secular, market-driven official pedagogic discourse'[6] which signals a weakening of and a relocation of the boundaries between the sacred and the profane. In this process, the relation between the knower and the known breaks down, knowledge becomes literally dehumanized and the very concept of education itself is placed in question.[7]

Whether plausible or not, this is a wonderful example of *fin de siècle* cultural pessimism – and he suspected that I might be arguing the opposite case. I had speculated on the implications of knowledge societies for breaking down boundaries between the production and the transmission of knowledge, and had argued that for the first time, the *principle* of constrained access to and distribution of knowledge and its legitimation was no longer a feasible basis for maintaining power relations and reproducing social inequalities. Castells makes much the same point when he argues that whilst being able to use new information and communication technologies is itself a source of power in 'societies of flows', this power simply cannot be sequestered. In such societies, there is no *prima facie* single and privileged source of information and knowledge, which 'itself is a flow, and no-one can survive in isolation from the flow'.[8] Global multimedia, he continued, construct and control the bridges between related but specialized universes of meanings and identities. One might even want to argue that these bridges are poised to take on the role of Basil's famous full stops, in a paradoxical cacophonous twist to those 'silent punctuations of social space which construct boundaries' and carry the message of power.[9]

The dissolution of boundaries *per se* and *tout court* is not the issue, but rather how these change their natures, roles and realizations under new conditions, most especially in relation to teaching and learning. Basil's ideas were predicated on an analysis of the changing reproduction of the social division of labour in the first modern era – in societies making the transition from mechanical to organic solidarity.[10] But it is at least conceivable, following this logic, that we confront a new and equally significant shift towards something beyond the organic model, something we could call 'network-based solidarit*ies*.' And if so, what would be the salient features? Who will be the paymasters, the veritable webmasters? What really changes, and what stays the same? The task, as Basil himself saw it, was to provide a language of description that resonates with this new era – and, of course, as he frequently thundered, this is just what is needed, for sociology is only too well-stocked with meta-theories that rarely concern themselves with the minutiae of the how. His theory, he concluded, had worked well enough for understanding pedagogic discourse as it was structured and realized two decades ago, but things had changed so much that he suspected it no longer fitted the bill. Retain the concepts, he advised, but construct a new elegant structure to house them.

Whilst the transitional period might suggest greater openness, the ultimate outcome, in his view, would be the positioning and use of knowledge and education to maintain boundaried terrains of acquisition, transmission and legitimation. The new marketized culture promotes a wholly imaginary and discursive modality that one might describe in terms of subjectivities that live on proverbial thin air, and whose characters suffer the corrosion posited by Richard Sennett.[11] In this scenario, the discourse of boundary dissolution is ultimately an illusion – whether we speak of opening up access, providing a plurality of routes to qualification and skill, or the integration of non-formal and informal learning processes as recognized contexts for acquisition and transmission, and much more besides. In reality, we are looking at the creation of a new hierarchy of privilege relayed through new modalities of regulation. The crucial element, for Basil, was the shaping of identity: the notion of trainability[12] requires the capacity for high contingency response in a risk-taking environment characterized by continuous change, that is, by inherent provisionality.

In order to explore these very provisional notions more systematically, we agreed to identify a range of key texts and contexts which might allow for a clearer identification of the processes, but equally the interests, involved. Three terrains came immediately to mind: the emergence of 'new higher education' against the background of the generally declining significance of the universities as vanguards of change; the 'dot.com' phenomenon as an example of potentially alternative routes to social mobility and biographical construction; and the official policy discourse emanating broadly from what has been called, rather reductively, the 'Blair–Schröder' alliance. Needless to say, the agenda remains a prospective one.

Basil always pointed out that his model did not necessarily assume that pedagogic communication occurs only in clearly defined and explicitly regulated environments called schools, colleges, training centres and universities. Nevertheless, almost all commentary and research around his theory have focused on precisely these. Yet, as he himself concluded, we are moving towards what he termed a 'totally pedagogised society' in which intentional teaching and learning has broken the bounds of both its material and its symbolic locations. Society becomes pedagogy, social relations become pedagogic relations.[13] In some sense, this was always so, just as every society has been in some sense a knowledge society. The difference lies in the move towards a systematically regulated social world in which all is instrumentalized in the service of the production and reproduction of economic and political power relations – and this time, in a globalized frame of reference.

That, of course, is precisely what Basil wrote in his contribution to the recent Lisbon conference dedicated to his work. He argued that we are moving towards a society different from but parallel to medieval Europe, in which religion, institutionalized in the shape of the Catholic Church, succeeded in creating and maintaining the first totally pedagogized society. Knowledge societies, for their part, will be regulated by the secular (super)state and pedagogically realized through lifelong learning, which is the device for producing and managing the flexibility and contingency demanded in the second modern era. Lifelong learning realizes the mobility of the subject, not only at the social and physical levels but, most crucially, at the levels of communication and identity.

This is precisely the reverse of the concept of the human subject in the first modern era and under the Christian Enlightenment concept of *Bildung*, which presupposes the essential and unique essence of each individual. Education in the sense of *Bildung* can and must foster the (self-)discovery and development of that essence. The essence of the human subject is not inherently malleable, but rather realizable through a bounded, but relatively open, process of (self-) learning. In other words, trainability had its limits – ultimately moral limits – based on respect for human dignity as a universal right of all individuals.

By contrast, this essence is today transformed, in Basil's conceptualization, into a vacuum – a malleable vacuum able and willing to be formed and reformed throughout life. Living in a vacuum is disorienting, and living on thin air certainly impossible, so temporary stabilities are provided through the commercial production and marketing of identities, both material and virtual. Paradoxically, we might conclude that the first modern era features a limited educational time and a bounded educational space for pedagogic communication whose outcomes should last a lifetime. Human subjects in the second modern era, on the other hand, will be expected to participate for the whole of their lives in repeated and boundless short-lived pedagogic intervals – because the vacuum is perpetually hungry for sustenance. In this sense, knowledge societies are not at all like mediaeval societies, which foresaw long-life pedagogy to create closed identities. Knowledge societies are interested in maintaining open identities on the basis of lifelong learning. Whether this is desirable or not, I leave to everyone's future reflection, including my own.

I would like to close by returning to some of the poetry we heard this morning. Rainer Maria Rilke was one of the greatest of the classical modern European poets, all of whom sought to resolve through their writing the metaphysical question of the meaning of life. The *Duineser Elegien* explore the issue of how it is possible to live when all the elements of knowing are ultimately beyond our ken. The metaphor of the child represents one of the borderline categories of existence between the knowable and the unknowable, the familiar and the strange. As we grow into being fully human, we cannot but lose touch with the unknowable and the strange. We agree to follow the rules of the human game, and life becomes a secure, fenced-in terrain of knowledge and experience – except, of course, that we are continually driven to transgress the boundaries, we seek to know what is beyond and unknowable. Human life is consecrated to the impossible goal of the rediscovery of the invisible.

I am convinced that Basil's particular appreciation of Rilke's writing is more than simply aesthetic, although that alone would be reason enough to admire his sensitivity. I think that some of Rilke's concerns resonate with Basil's own approach to understanding the world and his place within it, not least in terms of his response to the problematics of contemporary change. Rilke saw modernity as characterized by 'an ever more rapid disappearance of so much that is visible, that will not be replaced'. 'We are,' he wrote to his translator in 1925, 'perhaps the last ones to have known such things. We have a responsibility not only to keep their memory alive but more importantly to retain their human and everyday sacral value.'[14]

The Elegies seek to persuade us of our role as the essential translators between the visible and the invisible, even though the outcomes of these efforts will never be accessible to us. As such, the Elegies comprise a figurative theory of transformation. In a truly memorable phrase from the same letter, Rilke writes 'we are the bees of the invisible' – and this, I submit, is a supremely fitting epitaph for Basil himself. He was, without doubt, an ineffable bee of the invisible. I, for one, would not disdain the role of one of the sociological drones that might profitably learn from his example.

Notes

1 'The educational and social implications of the transition to knowledge societies in Europe', in Otto von der Gablentz et al. (eds) (2000) *Education 2020: Adapting to a changing world* (Baden-Baden: Nomos), pp. 75–90.

2 Even Manuel Castells' trilogy on *The Information Age* (1996–98)(Cambridge, MA: Blackwell) hardly mentions education, and certainly not sui generis; nor does his otherwise excellent essay 'Flows, networks and identities: a critical theory of the Informational Society', published in M. Castells et al. (eds) (1999) *Critical Education in the New Information Age* (Lanham/Boulder/New York/Oxford: Rowman and Littlefield), ch. 1. (The volume's essays were originally published in Spanish in 1994.)

3 Via the 1995 *White Paper Teaching and Learning – towards the learning society* (Brussels/ Luxembourg) and subsequently in a series of policy documents, culminating most recently in the European Commission's *Memorandum on Lifelong Learning* (Ref. SEC(2000)1830).

4 Basil Bernstein (2000) *Pedagogy, Symbolic Control and Identity: Theory, research, critique*, revised edition (Lanham/Boulder/New York/Oxford: Rowman and Littlefield), p. xxv.

5 As indicated explicitly by Joseph Solomos in his commentary to the interview conducted with Basil Bernstein in 1996 and published in the revised edition of *Pedagogy, Symbolic Control and Identity*; implicitly, Michael Apple makes very much the same point in *Official Knowledge: Democratic education in a conservative age* (2000, 2nd edition) (New York/London: Routledge), pp. 62–6.

6 Bernstein, *Pedagogy, Symbolic Control and Identity*, p. 77.

7 ibid., p. 86.

8 Castells, *Critical Education in the New Information Age*, pp. 49, 60. For empirical informa-

tion on the projected development of the NICT domain, see the Institute for Prospective Technological Studies Futures Report *Employment Map: Jobs, Skill and Working Life on the Road to 2010* (K. Ducatel and J.C. Burgelman, Series No. 13, EUR 19033, Seville, December 1999).

9   Bernstein, *Pedagogy, Symbolic Control and Identity*, pp. xiii, 7.

10 Paul Atkinson's *Language, Structure and Reproduction: An introduction to the sociology of Basil Bernstein* (1985) (London: Methuen), p. 36 admirably crystallizes the point; the summary provided by R.A. Morrow and C.A. Torres in *Social Theory and Education: A critique of theories of social and cultural reproduction* (1995) (New York: SUNY Press), pp. 190–201 draws substantially on Atkinson's analysis.

11 R. Sennett (1998) *The Corrosion of Character: The personal consequences of work in the new capitalism* (New York/London: W.W. Norton and Company).

12 Bernstein, *Pedagogy, Symbolic Control and Identity*, pp. 58–9.

13 In Ramón Flecha's piercing words: 'the official curriculum generates an engineering mentality that regiments the lifeworld. Even the most intimate and recreational areas of an individual's life can be colonised by invasive, totalising practices in the form of institutionalised courses of ballroom dancing, massage, or even flirting and kissing' ('New educational inequalities', in M. Castells *et al.* (eds) (1999), p. 69.

14 Cited in M. Engel and U. Fülleborn's commentary to the *Duineser Elegien* (2000) (Frankfurt a. M./Leipzig: Insel Verlag), p. 105; this now famous letter, dated 13 November 1925, was addressed to his translator Witold Hulewicz.

HOMAGE FROM CHILE TO PROFESSOR BASIL BERNSTEIN

Dear Marion; dear Saul and Francis; dear friends and colleagues,

We have come to this celebration of Basil's life from very far away. We have come from across the Atlantic and across the Andes, from the far south of the Southern Hemisphere.

We often wonder with amazement how it happened that a professor from the East of London came into our lives and had such an impact on our vision and our thoughts about ourselves and the world.

Dear Basil,

We have come here today to the Institute and the people to whom you gave the most of yourself, to tell them about your love for Chile and for us; about your generosity and about your courage; about your well hidden romanticism and the strength of your loyalties; about your sense of the sacred.

And we have come to tell them of our loyalty and our love for you, too.

They all know about your intellectual brilliance: about your being a seer; about your genius with language and meanings. We want to tell them about Basil in the South: Basil and the rural poor, the Church, government; Bernstein in Chile, Columbia and Argentina. But mainly in Chile. A Bernstein they probably never knew existed.

Friends,

We want to share with you our deep and immense and sincere thanks for the extraordinary gift of having had Basil as our mentor and maestro; our beloved tutor and counsellor; critic and teacher; accomplice and colluder in schemes and inventions and fantasies, as well as serious designs and constructions. He was influential and constructive in what we think were good designs for the building of institutions and programmes in education. But not only in education, in every activity we have undertaken since, Basil has influenced us.

He came down to remote Chile many times, in tough and dreadful times, when, as he used to say, the knock at the door could mean tragedy and horror. He always used to ask – what will you do when the knock at the door comes? With us, he always struck at the heart of things. And for Basil, who could be a dazzling juggler of words and symbols, a comedian and a joker, that heart of things was never a game; it was deadly serious. He didn't forget for a second his position in the dramas and tragedies of his century.

But he also came down to Chile after the dictatorship, in more peaceful and hopeful times: at times when many of us, his friends, were in government and had a say in the shaping of the country's future. He was then no less tough on us, though. The optimism of the 'young in power', he scathingly commented once, reminding us of the need for total commitment to our responsibilities and total detachment from the enchantment of power; of the need to be questioning and not complacent, ever. He was demanding – intellectually, morally and effectively. Always.

That was part of his gift to us. It was also the deal. No concessions of any kind. Ever. He gave it all to us; we demanded it all from him.

Twice we travelled with him to the rural countryside in the foothills of the Andes. He marvelled at the skill, toughness and generous naturalness with which his peasant companions accepted – his words – 'the first Jewish *huaso* in history'.[1]

Why did he love Chile? Why did he give so much generosity and time to us? The most distant corner of Latin America? Remote, proud, tragic, underdeveloped country?

We don't know for sure. But we have a few hunches. He was a deeply political man. He was part of a generation who fought in the cruellest war on ideological grounds. He was enlisted before the age of consent, to fight Nazism. He was a man for whom the relationship between his faith and Christianity was central and generative, not only for his own existential position, but also as a sociologist who enquired relentlessly into the nature of the relationship between social bonds and the sacred. We think that from both strands of his identity, Chile appealed to him. These Catholics and socialists from the south fighting Pinochet, asking questions and addressing issues that he found answers to earlier on – maybe that was the starting point of it all.

He taught us that love had to be fought for and conquered and cared for every day. He told us that Marion once said to him: '*Go to bloody Chile and get well.*' We now want to tell Marion and you all, that if he ever got well with us, we think it was through his committed involvement in something that he felt deeply about and judged important, even transcendental, sharing everything that he was with us: his wisdom; his devastating irony; his total respect for hard work and rigour; his inventiveness and humour; his patience and stubbornness; his moving loyalty and love for us, for our struggle, for our country.

He is one of us. He always will be.

All of us wanted to come here and share with you – Londoners, scholars from the University of London, scholars from other universities and other parts of the world, educators, colleagues and friends – that Basil, Professor Basil Bernstein, was a mentor, our mentor; a master; a friend and comrade: one of us. We consider that a valued privilege. A gift. We do not have the means to reciprocate to Marion, to Saul and Francis, or to this institution, his university – to some of us our university – our debt to Basil.

He influenced us. He worked at influencing us. Deeply, generatively. He loved us, our country, our people, our land. We miss him and mourn him. But it comforts us that through us and our work, he will live on in Chile for many years to come.

Christian Cox, Head of the Curriculum and Evaluation Unit, Ministry of Education, Chile.

Rosita Puga, teacher and Head of the Education Programme, Fundación Belén, Arzobispado de Santiago, Chile.

Catherine Kenrick, Head of International Co-operation, National Commission for the Environment, Government of Chile and Joint Co-ordinator of the National Botanic Garden of Chile.

José Joaquín Brunner, former Minister, Government of Chile, 1994–1998; currently Head of the Education Programme, Fundación Chile.

Marta Almarza, painter, Santiago, Chile.

Rev'd Patricio Cariola, S.J., former Director of CIDE (Centro de Investigación y Desarrollo de la Educación), Santiago, Chile.

Marianela Cerri, former researcher at CIDE, currently vice co-ordinator of the Curriculum and Evaluation Unit, Ministry of Education, Chile.

Viola Espínola, Education Expert, Interamerican Development Bank (IADB) Washington, D.C.

Jorge Fontaine, farmer and landowner, Pirque, Región Metropolitana, Chile.

Francisco Gazitúa, sculptor, former lecturer at St Martin's School of Arts, London; currently in Santiago, Chile.

Elena García-Huidobro, rural school primary teacher, Chincolco, V Region, Chile.

Jacqueline Gysling, former researcher at the CIDE Centre, currently Head of Curriculum, Primary Education, Ministry of Education, Chile.

Dr Antonio Infante, doctor, public health expert, former Head of Junta Auxilio Escolar y Becas, Ministry of Education, Chile.

Abraham Magendzo, Professor, Programme for Interdisciplinary Research in Education (PIIE), Catholic University, Santiago, Chile.

Sergio Martinic, Director of CIDE, Santiago, Chile.

Raimundo Prado, farmer and landowner, Chincolco, V Region, Chile.

Gastón Sepúlveda, Professor of Education, Universidad de la Frontera, Temuco, Chile.

Rev'd John Swope, S.J., former Director of CIDE (1995–2000); currently Executive Director of the Secretariat of the Church of Latin America of the National Conference of Catholic Bishops of the United States, Washington.

Note
1 *Huaso* is a central cultural category in rural Chile. Man on horseback.

IS THERE A 'SOCIAL DEVICE'?

A reflection on the work of Basil Bernstein

Bill Hillier, Professor of Architectural and
Urban Morphology and Chairman of the Bartlett School
of Graduate Studies, University College London

IN HIS 'Pedagogic codes and their modalities of practice' (Bernstein 1996) Basil Bernstein warns us: 'members share a common recognition rule which orientates the members to the speciality of this context.... Members not sharing that common pedagogic communication may well remain silent or offer what other members would consider inappropriate talk and conduct'. I may well be about to do that. I am not a sociologist or sociolinguist. I study space: how human activity and thought organizes space and creates the spatial conditions in which we live. I am surprised and delighted to be here. My main qualification is, I believe, that I used to talk to Basil. What I will talk about here is what we used to talk about and what I would say now if we were able to talk again.

I have a guilty legacy from Basil. A few years ago, after an evening of talking, he suggested I borrow what seemed an unlikely book: Soren Kirkegaard's *Concluding Unscientific Postscript*. I puzzled over this for a long while, but eventually found this:

> Because abstract thought is *sub specie aeterni* it ignores the concrete and the temporal, the existential process, the predicament of the existing individual arising from his being a synthesis of the temporal and the eternal situated in existence. Now if we assume that abstract thought is the highest manifestation of human activity, it follows that philosophy and the philosophers proudly desert existence, leaving the rest of us to face the worst. And

something else, too, follows for the abstract thinker, namely that since he is an existing individual he must in some way or another be suffering from absentmindedness.

The abstract problem of reality (if it is permissible to treat this problem abstractly, the particular and the accidental being constituents of the real, and directly opposed to abstraction) is not nearly so difficult a problem as it is to raise and answer the question of what it means that this definite something is a reality. This definite something is just what abstract thought abstracts from. But the difficulty lies in bringing this definite something and the ideality of thought together, by penetrating the concrete particularity with thought.   (Kierkegaard 1941: 267

More than any other sociologist, Basil 'penetrated the concrete particularity with thought'. He showed how the materiality of everyday life is pervaded by the large-scale abstractions we call society. It was a shared interest in the materiality of the social world we live in and the abstractions which seem to govern it that we talked about. It gave Basil a profound interest in space, both as an object of analysis and as a set of metaphors for his theoretical work. From my point of view, his theories have a profound spatiality.

I was first attracted to his work by the concept of code: systems of space, like classrooms, are structured by systematic abstractions through which material patterns take on a social meaning. I shared his belief in the central role of description – or theoretical description as I prefer to call it – in research: that is, the attempt to characterize real situations in terms of the abstract models which seem to impose their patterns on them.

I think two aspects of my work interested Basil. First, I believed that what I called the 'social logic of space' was underpinned by a prior logic of possibilities, so that society constructed space through the intermediary of a set of possible pathways which could be mapped (Hillier and Hanson 1984). With the hindsight of Basil's later concept of the 'pedagogic device' (Bernstein 1996), I could now call this a 'spatial device' since its defines not a code but a system of possible codes. Every society uses the 'spatial device' in some variant to realize itself in space, and exogenous factors like changes in technology affect space through the intermediary of the 'spatial device'.

The second idea which I think he found interesting was the role of randomness in the models that I and my colleagues were developing to map the variability of social space. We conceptualized spatial order as restrictions on an underlying random process, so there could be different degrees as well as different types of order, and different amounts of randomness would be present in different situations. This meant that that different space codes could formally carry different amounts of social baggage as well at least carry it in very different ways.

When we talked, we did not talk about the sociology of education, or about space, but about the relations between our theories. Each was trying to do what the other did not. He was showing how much of society, the big beast, could be crammed into the classroom, changing our ideas about what constituted the micro and macro in society. We were mapping fields of possibility, and we had our eye on our own smaller beast, the city, which like society seemed to emerge from large number of micro-situations without our designing it or understanding it. Both our positions led us to the same puzzle: the nature of society itself, the big beast whose shadows he saw in the classroom like the shadows in Plato's cave, and which we saw in its spatial outputs.

Basil was never a 'social system' theorist but, as time went by, I believe he became more and more interested in the big beast, raising his gaze from the classroom and the family to try to describe what it was whose shadows appeared there. I see much of his later work as an attempt to find a way out of the cave and confront society itself. The notion of the 'pedagogic device' is, I believe, a key crystallization of this. The pedagogic device is the family of possible structures that turn institutional patterns into consciousness. It defines the ways in which institutional differences *become* ways of thinking and acting in the social world. As such, it provides, as Basil says, 'a symbolic rule for consciousness'. Basil compares the 'pedagogic device' to the 'linguistic device', and points to its religious (in the Durkheimian rather than Aquinian sense) origins. He then uses it to offer morphological comparison between different kinds of society. Basil is, I suggest, beginning to look at the social DNA, the informational stuff embedded in institutional patterns that govern the everyday production and reproduction of social life. The concept of pedagogy has been generalized to the apparatus of social reproduction itself. In spite of Basil's modesty in the matter (Bernstein 1996: xxvi), he is now talking about society.

I find inherent in this one of the most interesting formulations yet for the great unanswered question at the heart of sociology: what on earth is society? The pedagogic device is close to being – or at least guides us towards – a general 'social device'. If we ever agree on a definition of society, I suspect it may include an answer to the question: is there a Bernsteinian 'social device'? If this sounds odd, let me embed it in two other pieces of theory into which I believe it fits snugly. The first is the Giddens concept of the 'duality of structure': that while 'virtual', structure is both the medium and the outcome of 'situated practices' in space-time and therefore links the production of social realities in space-time to the reproduction of their structures (Giddens 1984). Basil is beginning to describe what a virtual structure might be like, what it is that is reproduced through space-time practices, and why we may expect it to differ from one society or time to another.

The second is from my own field and suggests how we might eventually see such apparently 'virtual' structures as real and measurable properties of space-time systems. It arises from a reconsideration of the spatial metaphors which so profoundly influenced the shape of Basil's theories, but which he increasingly suspected defined limits as well as possibilities (Bernstein 1996: xiii). Basil's guiding metaphors were – as he himself says – spatial notions of 'boundary', which he specifies as 'inside/outside, intimacy/distance, here/there, near/far, us/them. These notions for the most part describe our perspective on and experience of space more than they describe space itself. In studying real space, we find that these notions get you into the problem, but don't get you out the other side. This is because space is *fundamentally* more complex and richer than these terms suggest: it is relational. I do not mean this in a Leibnizian sense, but in the sense that space does not exist for us as discrete elements but as a continuous system of interrelatedness shaped by and shaping the way we live. In space, the pattern is the thing, much more than the elements that make up the pattern

The profound relationality of space is shown even in the simple spatial terms (prepositions) that are found in all languages and which are a vital part of its ability to picture the world: between, inside, through, beyond, among, and so on (Bloom *et al.* 1996). But these terms deal for the most part with spatial relations between two or three things. As such they map an elementary spatial gestuary which reflect the means by which we cognize the space around us. But they do not give us a handle on the emergent properties of the much richer and more complex systems of space which are constructed out of this gestuary. What we find we need in studying space is a configurational language, related to the elementary gestuary, but actually characterized by being able to describe relations between each element and all the others in the system in a numerical way, even when they are not directly connected to each other (Hillier 1996).

For space, the configurational language is constructible by the improbable manoeuvre of disentangling space from its embedding in the social and material world and treating it as a thing in itself by representing is as a very large graph. Once we do this we discover patterns of relationality in space itself which are the result of social processes working themselves out in the material world, but which can only be seen when space is treated on its own, as pure configuration. Once identified, the patterns can then be re-embedded in the social processes that construct them, thus allowing us to discern both social causes and consequences of the patterns.

Used in this way, configurational languages have proved so powerful in understanding structure and function in complex systems of space like cities, that we conclude that seen as space entities like cities are 'strongly relational systems', that is systems in which the relations of each element to all others are more important for the structure and functioning of the system than intrinsic or virtual properties of the elements themselves. This is why such systems can be usefully conceptualized and analysed as very large graphs using configurational measures which relate elements of the graph together however remote from each other they may be within the graph. The concept of a strongly relational system allows us to show that a set of space-time events which cannot be seen all at once can nevertheless be shown to be real space-time systems with 'configurational' structures which are intrinsic to them, and which mediate their relations to other domains.

What is the relevance of this to Basil's work? What I would like to have suggested to Basil is that there is a strongly relational system somewhere close to the heart of what we mean by society. What I am thinking is this. If we follow Giddens' reasoning, we see structure in social systems as 'virtual' because we find evidence for its existence only in dispersed practices, in the same way that we find evidence of language structure in discrete linguistic acts. This makes structure look rather weak, little more than rule following. In fact, the cautious view of space-time that leads Giddens to this conclusion seems unnecessary. Although situated practices appear as discrete events, none can exist in space-time isolation and no collection is likely to form a discrete system, because memberships are shared and individuals pass continuously from one to another. Seen in a time perspective, situated practices constitute a continuous system of time-space relatedness. On reflection, in fact, it seems likely that the existence of such a system is one of the preconditions for what we name as a society. It is exactly this kind of global – if largely indirect – relatedness that can be conceptualized as a strongly relational system and therefore could in principle (though only in practice with prohibitive effort) be represented as a very large graph and analysed using configurational measures.

Now because this large graph is the dependent variable of a continuous process of social construction it is likely that, as with the city, its structures – its 'genotypes' as we say of such graphs in the study of space – are in some sense configurational imprints of the social forces that have created it. For example, Durkheimian 'mechanical' and 'organic' solidarities would construct quite different patterns in the graph. Through recursive activity, these structures would be reproduced, and thus becoming part of the means by which the social forces were reproduced. The difference is that now the structures are not virtual, but potentially mappable properties of a real space-time system. Through the concept of the strongly relational system we find a space-time link between the social realities of situations and the virtualities of the social macro-system.

We may then use the concept to link Bernstein and Giddens. The pattern of remoteness and nearness in the graph of the system would both reflect the structuring activity of the Bernsteinian social device and be reproduced Giddens-wise through the recursivities of space-time activity. The Bernsteinian 'social device' thus appears as the core link, the social DNA, which acts as the informational intermediary between the forces shaping society – technological, economic, and so on – and the actual forms of global relatedness that we find at the core of society. Society, we might conjecture, is a strongly relational system, shaped by the social device and reproduced through its space-time realizations. How we live in space-time is how we understand it, and how we understand it is how it makes us in its image.

These are of course wild speculations. But they are in the spirit of my conversations with Basil. One of our last conversations took place in somewhat improbable circumstances, but circumstances nonetheless that remind us of the unexpected proximity of situated practices in the space-time of society. I had not seen Basil for some time and we met by chance one morning in Torrington Place. We talked for a few minutes about what each had been doing, and agreed it was good to talk at greater length, but in about two weeks, he said, because he was going abroad. I said I was too, and we agreed to call each other on our return. Three days later I walked into my small hotel in a side street in downtown Santiago in Chile, and saw Basil sitting in the entrance hall. I am proud to say we resumed our conversation without any reference to the improbability of this encounter, and for the next few mornings we conversed over fruit juice and coffee. This encounter was so unlikely, that it leads me to entertain the irrational hope that one day we may talk again. That would be a surprise. But it would be the best surprise.

References

Bernstein, B. (1996) *Pedagogy, Symbolic Control and Identity.* London: Taylor and Francis.

Bloom, P., Petersen, M., Nadel, L. and Garrett, M. (1996) *Language and Space.* Cambridge, MA: MIT Press.

Giddens, A. (1984) *The Constitution of Society.* London: Polity Press.

Hillier, B. and Hanson, J. (1984) *The Social Logic of Space.* Cambridge: Cambridge University Press.

Hillier, B. (1996) *Space is the Machine.* Cambridge: Cambridge University Press.

Kierkegaard, S. (1941) *Concluding Unscientific Postscript.* (Trans. D. Swenson and W. Lowrie) Princeton: Princeton University Press, p. 267. (Originally in Danish.)

AN APPLICATION OF BASIL BERNSTEIN'S CONSTRUCTS OF 'VISIBLE AND INVISIBLE PEDAGOGIES'

Courtney B. Cazden, Charles William Eliot
Professor of Education Emerita, Harvard University

BASIL BERNSTEIN HAS BEEN a special mentor since I first encountered his early writings in 1963 while preparing a graduate student assignment (subsequently Cazden 1966) and then met him and Marion in the tumultuous spring of May 1968. I have a flashbulb memory of sitting in my tiny office in fall 1967 as a recently certified assistant professor and hearing his voice on the trans-Atlantic phone inviting me to my first international conference held at the CIBA foundation here in London. At that conference, Jack Tizard invited me to write about Basil's work on child language for a developmental journal he edited (Cazden 1968).

More important to me in the longer run than these still vivid personal memories is the overall correspondence between certain phases of our respective careers: teaching working-class children before moving to the university; beginning research in the early 1960s (Basil in the late 1950s) with a focus on social class differences in children's primary language socialization; and subsequently shifting back to the classroom in work on 'pedagogic discourse'. In these brief comments, I will exemplify my use of Basil's ideas in the American educational context, and then at the end raise a question for future exploration about his concept of 'codes'.

The visible and invisible pedagogies of Reading Recovery
US school reform rhetoric about educating all students for the flexible appli-

cation of high-level skills clashes with the reality of continued massive social class and colour (ethnicity/race) differences in school achievement. While there are many sources of macro-structural inequality, within the classroom one has to ask how – theoretically and practically – one can teach towards flexible competencies through explicit teaching. In trying to understand this seeming paradox in more than an ad hoc way, especially in literacy teaching where pedagogical controversies are most unproductively heated, I have turned to Basil's distinction between Visible and Invisible Pedagogy (VP and IP). While I am sure Basil has often been critical of my naggingly practical objectives, he has been unfailingly generous in our periodic conversations over lunch at the Tavistock or in his closet-size retirement office.

Here, for example, is my 'Bernsteinian' analysis in outline form of the features of Reading Recovery, a one-to-one tutorial programme imported into both the US and England from New Zealand, for the lowest achieving young children (from Cazden 1999).

VP features
Classification
Strong within-school as child is taken to a separate room with a separate teacher and a special curriculum, all different from the regular classroom.

Framing
Strong pacing in the acceptance of a goal of independent reading by the end of first grade, and in little time for chat within the 30-minute lessons.

Strong in the teacher selection of a new book to be read each day; in teaching monitoring and reinforcement of reading and writing strategies that are the theoretical core of instructional design; strong in clear criteria of book difficulty and strategy repertoire that children must meet before being 'discontinued' from the programme.

IP features
Framing
Weakened through the individualization of the programme for each child: in the sequence of new books introduced; the sequence of strategies and of sounds, letters, words that are called to the child's attention; and the number of weeks (a more macro aspect of pacing) that each child remains in the daily programme.

Although in the daily writing segment, framing is strong through criteria of correct (not invented) spelling, framing is weakened in topic and word choice by the child's oral composition of the text to be transcribed into writing.

Classification

Weakened school/home classification in two ways. Each day, teacher writes the child's written sentence on a sentence strip and cuts into pieces which, along with well-read little books, go home to be read to 'Mum'. Also, parents are encouraged to come to school to observe one or more lessons with their child.

Describing a specific programme in the terms of a strong theory like Basil's can be more than an exercise in re-naming. In can suggest new questions about the programme itself and hypotheses about dimensions of generalizability across specific programmes.

Within Reading Recovery: what about 'regulative discourse' in which, according to the theory, 'instructional discourse' is always embedded. 'Regulative discourse refers to modes of conduct. For the learners it must be enabling, helping them to find a voice. It requires adaptation in cultural, including bodily, ways' (paraphrased from my notes, personal communication January 1995). Do the most successful Reading Recovery teachers adapt intuitively in such ways?

Across programmes: Bernstein's first (1975) chapter on VP/IP reads as strong rationale for the benefits of VP for working-class students. But the second, written during the Thatcher years (and perhaps drawing on his own early teaching experiences?), suggests the benefits of what I am calling a 'mixed system':

> a visible pedagogy which would weaken the relation between social class and educational achievement [may well] require a supportive preschool structure, a relaxation of the framing on pacing and sequencing rules, and a weakening of the framing regulating the flow of communication between the school classroom and community(ies) the school draws upon.
>
> (Bernstein 1990: 79)

The empirical study of science education by Morais and her colleagues in Lisbon (1992), which Basil has called 'a fundamental exploration of the usefulness of the [i.e. his] theory', can also be read as an example of a mixed system in the unexpected success of the pedagogical practice intermediate between VP and IP extremes, especially for the initially lowest students. Strong theory should help us find and/or design other such successful programmes.

A question about 'codes'

As Basil was all too painfully aware, his early research on children's primary language socialization into 'restricted' and 'elaborated' codes was widely criticized in the United States. His time with us ran out before I had the chance to discuss with him a current US theory that bears intriguing resemblance to his: James Gee's theory of 'primary and secondary Discourses' [capital *D* in the original] that has avoided most (not all) such criticisms. Volumes by the two are joined in simultaneous publication in Allen Luke's series on 'Critical perspectives on literacy and education' for Taylor and Francis (Bernstein 1996; Gee 1996). My next self-assessment is to try to understand better aspects of the two theories and of the contexts of their contrasting receptions in the 1960s and 1990s respectively.

References

Bernstein, B. (1975) *Class, Codes and Control: Vol. 3: Towards a theory of educational transmissions*. London: Routledge and Kegan Paul.

Bernstein, B. (1990) *Class, Codes and Control: Vol. 4: The Structuring of Pedagogic Discourse*. London: Routledge.

Bernstein, B. (1996) *Pedagogy, Symbolic Control and Identity*. London and Bristol, PA: Taylor and Francis.

Cazden, C.B. (1966) 'Subcultural differences in child language: an interdisciplinary review', *Merrill-Palmer Quarterly of Behavior and Development* 12, 185–219.

Cazden, C.B. (1968) 'Three sociolinguistic views of the language and speech of lower-class children – with special attention to the work of Basil Bernstein', *Developmental Medicine and Child Neurology* 600–12.

Cazden, C.B. (1999) 'The visible and invisible pedagogies of Reading Recovery', in A.J. Watson and L.R. Giocelli (eds) *Accepting the Literacy Challenge*. Sydney: Scholastic Australia: 62–71.

Gee, J.P. (1996) *Social Linguistics and Literacies: Ideology in Discourses* (2nd edition). London and Bristol, PA: Taylor and Francis.

Morais, A., Fontinhas, F. and Neves, I. (1992) 'Recognition and realization rules in acquiring school science – the contribution of pedagogy and social background of students', *British Journal of Sociology of Education* 13: 247–71.

A TRIBUTE

Gunther Kress, Professor of Education,
Institute of Education, University of London

BASIL BERNSTEIN was not a linguist, and yet he provided the means for decisive insight into the principles of the organization of language in use. This was based on a simple proposition, namely that users of language, in their everyday actions, organize the resources of language to achieve the ends posed by the demands of their social lives. These demands follow the lines and principles of the organization of the social groups in which their everyday lives have their location. Hence the organization of language as *code* both as the expression of the real actions of individuals in their social places, and as the expression of the organization of their social groups.

The proposition was not itself new: it was there in the work of Michael Halliday with whom Bernstein had begun a regular collaboration at that time, and it had been there in the work of earlier British and other European linguists, notably the work of Buehler, and of course in the work of the Soviet linguists, 'discovered' in the West in the mid-1970s. However, in the writings of Bernstein it was articulated with such clarity, supported by extensive, detailed empirical research, that it proved impossible to ignore as just another view of language. It was either overwhelmingly plausible – as it was for me – or it proved an unpalatable and unspeakable truth. The latter turned out to be the overwhelming response, whether for the formalist, structuralist and psychologistic American mainstream, or for those on the 'left' politically. For the former it proved an impossible truth for a number of reasons: it made the social at least seemingly prior to the psychological; it counterposed to the abstraction of 'language as such' the reality of the many differently organized codal forms of language; it challenged the autonomy of language, and thus the autonomy of linguistics as a discipline. Above all it asserted the reality of linguistic form: and it was that which made it equally or even more difficult for those whose political convictions placed them on the side of those who occupied the lower reaches of a class-ridden society. For them it was impossible as a truth because it seemed to confirm those whose social class position was already difficult as 'lesser' also in respect to the expressive means which were seen to define articulateness, rationality, a full humanity.

Hence it produced responses, from the 'left' as from the 'right', that in the end remained facile even if well-intentioned: focused on the immediate, unable or unwilling to confront the deep challenge posed by Bernstein's hypotheses, theoretically and politically.

Despite this overt rejection, these ideas have had the profoundest impact, both on understandings of language, and in their effect on ideas about learning. For Hallidayan linguists in particular, the notion of code has been very significant through the concept of coding-orientation: the relatively stable (even if changing over time) arrangements of the linguistic resources within a group, corresponding to the foregrounded and stable practices of that group. The individual meets language not 'as such', but in the form of these coding-orientations, which facilitate certain forms and arrangements. Thus those inhabiting different coding-orientations have different givens – themselves encoding social practices – facilitated, and it is these facilitated arrangements which already provide representational and conceptual orientations for their users.

The significance both for learning and for what is to be learned is clear. What is to be learned will have specific form depending on its representation through codes of different kinds. These codes will also shape how what is to be learned will be learned: habits of conceptual engagement leading to habits of cognitive work. Above all, the realist notions of signs – to put this now semiotically – the codal arrangements as signs having the form they do because of the meanings that they realize, bestows agency on learners. The language-as-code user is a language-as-code reshaper; (s)he has agency in relation to the resources of representation. The learner is the reshaper of the resources both for her/himself – remaking the inner representations as the outward representations are remade; but this happens with signs which have themselves been shaped in this way. The sign – of whatever kind – carries in its shape and in its materiality the traces of the conditions of its making. It carries these forward to its reading and to its next remaking, in reading and in the next outward making.

Acting with the resources of language is therefore always representing the shape of the social givens, and (re)shaping them at the same time, reconstituting not only the resources of representation but also the individual and the social givens.

Codes are therefore the effects of real human action in the environments in which the action takes place. The theory of codes provided a means of understanding semiotic systems (potentially of all kinds – as was clear for Bernstein in his later work, on 'discourse' for instance) as the effects of real agency, and of the conditions of the production of the sign.

This is and remains important now, when communicational conditions are in deep transition: language, for instance, no longer the only nor often the central representational and communicational mode, and the media of communication also in the process of foundational shift. The screen is the contemporaneously dominant site – even if at the moment only as the imagined dominant site – of representation and communication, with its multiple modes of representation simultaneously available and used.

In hindsight it is clear that Bernstein's theory of communication, that of codes foremost, has always been a thoroughly semiotic theory, a theory of semiosis in which agency is central as the shaping force of the system. The theory of 'discourse' as elaborated by him provides the means of connecting the social to the minutiae of the realizational, in any mode, and at any level of abstraction. The principles of representation and communication which he enunciated in the theory of codes stands now as a general theory of semiosis: namely that the conditions that obtain in the making of the sign shape the forms of the sign. And so the categories and hypotheses which Bernstein elaborated, coming out of the high era of structuralism (and Marxism) will, I am certain, stand up in the present, with its new communicational arrangements, its fragmenting social arrangements, and its as yet quite uncertain new framings. Indeed, I feel certain that they will be more essential for providing accounts for that period than they might have been in the more stable past.

BERNSTEIN'S SOCIOLOGY OF PEDAGOGY

A feminist tribute

Madeleine Arnot, School of Education and Jesus College, University of Cambridge

BASIL BERNSTEIN WAS THE first to accept that concerns about gender were not the focus of his theory. He would also be the first to admit that neither gender or feminist theory had much direct effect on his work, not so much because of lack of interest but because of the level at which the theory worked. He worried about what he called 'the inevitability' of such theory in its understandings and social projections. Gender relations, he understood, were the consequences of the social order not the cause.

Yet in an extraordinary way, precisely because his theory offered an abstract exploration of the generative principles underlying the social order, its classifications and forms of regulation and reproduction, it could be used to describe and analyse the ambiguities and specializations associated with women's positioning in society. Women's position of power but also their subordination played a central role in his theory of education. Although understated, Bernstein's sociology highlighted, in various important and insightful ways, women's position within what he called the field of symbolic control. As educators, women as mothers and as teachers were deeply implicated in his accounts of pedagogic discourses, language, identity and control. The gender stratification of higher education he also described as shaping men's and women's access to different types of discourse and their potential within it.

Bernstein's theory of pedagogy has played a fascinating role in the development of gender theory in sociological studies of education. There is now an international group of feminist academics who have chosen to position themselves within the male defined and controlled intellectual field by engaging with Bernstein's theoretical project – an exploration of the modes of educational transmission. There are also female scholars who would not necessarily wish to be labelled as feminist yet have used Bernstein's theory to explore gender relations and difference in the family and various educational contexts. Female theorists of pedagogy, too, have drawn upon Bernstein's conceptual framework or research problematic.

A year before his death Basil Bernstein helped me contact this small but highly selected group of academics in countries as culturally diverse as Australia, Colombia, Japan, Portugal, Spain, South Africa, the UK and the USA. Many of the group had been his graduates in the past but had now become colleagues. My task was to discover the nature of women's engagement with his theoretical work – a task never before attempted and which proved to be highly rewarding. It revealed in a vivid way, the conceptual positioning and recontextualizing of his theory and the personal meanings ascribed to it. Above all it demonstrated how wide-ranging were the possibilities for developing his theoretical project.

The extraordinary power of Bernstein's sociology of pedagogy over-rides to some extent the concerns of feminists about male-centred academic discourses that make claims to knowledge about women and for women. His use of dichotomous structuralisms appears to be far removed from the connectedness and integration associated with female experience. Yet at the same time his work has played a key role in theories of gender and schooling. Two major reasons explain the attraction of his theory: its *explanatory* power, which is linked to its *universalistic* but also its *transgressive* nature, and, secondly its *educative/transformative* power.

The explanatory power of Bernstein's sociology of pedagogy has been sufficient justification for its use in constructing gender theory. Even if it could not be simplified into programmatic strategies, the purposes of such theory could be related to feminist political agendas. For many of the women academics I questioned, the mastery of powerful explanatory discourses, generating *independent* and *universalistic* forms of knowledge (a disconnection rather than a dependence on social and political frameworks) appears to be precisely the basis of attraction.

Drawing upon Durkheimian traditions, Bernstein argued that the mixing of categories are precisely the points of danger and transition, a weakening of the borders between the sacred and the profane. Bernstein might well have been talking about the ambivalent positioning of his own work in the interstices between sociological, educational and socio-linguistic theory. Recently he proudly remarked that his explorations of a sociology of pedagogy were characterized precisely by the absence of a field of study or professional identification This transgressive positioning made it difficult to locate him simply within fashionable intellectual categorizations or fields of study. His unique combination of the concepts of power and control as guiding principles of all forms of educational transmission meant that he was able to integrate macro and micro sociological concepts and to appeal, latterly, for the importance of an analysis which integrated structure, culture, language and discourse.

The ambivalence of Bernstein's theory in its continuing forms turns readers into pedagogical subjects. It encourages active and continual engagement with the text. It encourages reflection, speaking directly to women's personal experience of being female and working class – both subordinate social categories – and to their experience of being mothers and teachers. At the same time, his theory offers female academics, positioned in the margins of various intellectual fields, the possibility of being repositioned within higher education through the mastery of his discourse. The personal and the positional appear to be inseparable elements of such female engagements with the Bernsteinian project. In his own inimitably humorous way, Bernstein himself described such engagements as involving the 'rebiographising the subject' where the 'subject emerges at the end, perhaps with an inner coherence or with a strong anti-transference or just thankful its over' (personal communication).

His theory also transforms male and female disciples into recontextualizers. Women academics (alongside men) have played a key role in developing and repositioning his work in an amazing range of intellectual fields and national contexts. Research has focused upon gender codes in education, women's role as mothers and educators, parent education, the gendering of pedagogical discources and pedadagic devices, critical feminist pedagogy, the construction of occupations in symbolic and material fields, class and gender identity forms, family modalities and school choices, and gender and literacy. Out of this work, too, comes a variety of suggestions for future gender research, some of which Bernstein himself advocated.

- The theory of pedagogic discourse suggests a continuing commitment to analyse at a deeper structuralist level how the structuring of pedagogic communication at macro and micro level shaped gender relations, identities, social types, and difference. Investigation into different code modalities differentiating along gender lines in pedagogic practice is of crucial importance. How do gender identities emerge in concrete practices, in specific social and political contexts, and how are such identities linked to institutional structures of social control? Research needs to investigate how different means/text articulations produce different patterns of subjectivity according to gender. Also, to what extent can Bernsteinian theory describe and interpret the processes of production, fixing and canalizing of desire of students and how students' internalized voices construct their own representations of gender?

- Research conducted on male and female youth, their orientations to schooling, the forms of class and gender resistance and the construction of gender divisions demonstrates the power of Bernstein's theory to codify and theorize experiential and perspectival data. These applications suggest important engagements with shifts in the forms of knowledge/discourse. Bernstein suggested that the feminist political movement has re-centred identities ('consummation of self' and 'rituals of inwardness') thus weakening resources for the construction of traditional stable identities. Do such shifts signify class fractions? And what are the relations within these generalized bases for resistance and the reorganization of capitalism and pedagogic discourses?

- Since the 1980s a strong feminist interest has developed in his theory of the new middle classes and women's position in different pedagogic developments. His emphasis upon women's domestic pedagogic work calls for more empirical investigation as does the continuing interest in exploring in more depth family cultures and structures, the structure of language and communication and the processes of class and gender reproduction. There is also an interest in using his theory of positional and personal family types to understand different class and gendered patterns of school choice, to account for the boundaries and negotiations between official vertical discourses and family-based horizontal pedagogic discourses.

- Are different forms of knowledge/discourse gendered? The sociological and historical investigation of the class and gendered nature of pedagogic discourses has only begun. Have particular pedagogies been associated with the different roles of women/mothers *within* social class groupings, with class fractions or with the domestication of women/students by depriving them of the mastery of powerful theoretical discourses?

- Bernstein saw the importance of researching the specific conditions which generate a male or female voice and how gender voices are constructed, made explicit and positioned in the intellectual field. His analysis of horizontal discourses suggests a negative association of feminism with 'pedagogic populism' (in the form of emancipatory integrative pedagogies) and the development of horizontal knowledge structures with weak grammars. Under what conditions can feminism adopt a more powerful vertical knowledge structure that generates theory before voice? What are the historical effects of feminist knowledge on the school system and what is the potential of feminist knowledge to become transformative of social power?

Female engagements with Bernstein's theory of pedagogy have been active, intellectual and powerful. Current gender research has, to some extent, been celebratory of Bernstein's work but it has also elaborated his theory and developed its applicability in relation to a range of gender issues. Gender relations and women's position within the educational system still remain under-theorized in his theory. The potential, however, is clearly there to develop feminist research and research on gender within the problematic of Bernstein's sociology of pedagogy.

BECOMING A RESEARCHER

Reflections on the pedagogic practices of
Basil Bernstein

Andrew Brown, Senior Lecturer in Research Methods,
Institute of Education, University of London

THE EMPHASIS THUS FAR in the day has, quite rightly, been on Basil's academic work, research and publications: the public aspects of his work. As one of Basil's many former research students, a number of whom are here today, I would like to spend the next few minutes reflecting upon Basil's work as a research student supervisor. This is an aspect of his work which was less visible to the wider academic community but was of great importance to him, to his students and to the Institute of Education and which clearly had far wider impact.

It is clear that Basil placed great value on working with research students. He always took care to acknowledge in his writing the students with whom he had been working. Indeed, he presented the second part of his last book as testament to his debt to his research students. I hope that I can, in a small way today, express something of our debt to him. As many of you will know, I was the last of Basil's students to complete in his lifetime (no great accolade – it just means that everyone else finished before me).

Since the large funded projects of Basil's Sociological Research Unit days, working with research students clearly played an important part in promoting and provoking the development of his ideas. Students brought to Basil a diverse range of research questions, theoretical preoccupations, empirical knots and sets of experiences that prompted him to address a range of new problems and to test and develop his thinking. In my own experience, and from conversations with others and, indeed, the written and spoken tributes people have offered today, Basil addressed the work of his students with tremendous seriousness and generosity. Supervision does not adequately describe either the relationship or the process. Basil approached the work in a spirit of collaboration. When I was working with him he wanted to meet once a week (at least). Each tutorial would last around two hours, often followed by lunch. Throughout the project he remained completely engaged with the research I was doing. He could always be relied on to tell me precisely, and in great detail, what my work was about in those moments, all too frequent, in which I had completely lost direction.

This might all seem like an excessive time commitment on the part of the tutor, especially considering that I was a part-time student. The issue of time was of vital importance to Basil and voiced clearly in his writing on the process of doing research. He was particularly concerned with the constraints placed on research students and tutors by what he called the 'new official research economy'. He saw pressures from government funding agencies for higher education and research as pushing universities to offer more with fewer resources, thus squeezing the opportunities available for student and tutor to work together and reducing the years available for completion. Efficiency was a taboo word for Basil (one of many – the inadvertent or careless use of one of these words could constitute the focus of an entire tutorial). When Basil took on the supervision of John Mace's PhD he made it a condition that John was not to mention efficiency in his work – a tall order for someone working in the field of economics.

Time was further squeezed by the developing view that the PhD was a form of professional training and the subsequent incorporation of taught components into the programme. This view that research degrees could provide some form of generic training and the curricularizing of the processes of research clearly represented to Basil a diminution of research and a challenge to the status of the discipline (any discipline, but his specific concern was always, of course, sociology). The view that, as he has said, the PhD is a form of driving licence rather than a licence to explore was one to be resisted because it rendered certain forms of work, particularly rigorous modes of analysis, untenable. In my own case, Basil was keenly aware that I was under pressure to complete. At the point at which I had finished my empirical work he declared, 'You now have the choice of whether to do it the quick way or the right way'. He was not really presenting the choice here – it had to be the right way. I am not clear that he knew what the quick way was. His rationale for 'doing it the right way' was, first, that if you did not you would not have anything to teach your own students and, second, that the first thing students would do would be to read their supervisor's thesis.

Meeting so frequently placed tremendous pressure on production of ideas and text. He would go through every piece of writing thoroughly, raising questions and making suggestions. This sometimes took the form of a lacerating critique of some, or even all, of one's work. This could be particularly harrowing and has been likened by Paul Dowling to being put through a mangle. As Paul observes in his tribute to Basil, Basil would always follow such an event with the question, 'Lunch?' For Basil it was the text that was under scrutiny not you. This separation is difficult to achieve and sustain (it was certainly difficult for Basil in his own work and relationships). I have to say that with heavy work and home demands it was often difficult for me to keep up with this intensity of engagement. I knew Basil's haunts and pathways around the Institute well and could if need be keep out of his way. It wouldn't take long, however, for an envelope with his distinctive writing to arrive in my tray – a terse, maybe sarcastic, invitation to get back in touch. Who last paid for lunch would be a key factor in the tenor of the message. Basil's induction into the use of email added whole new dimension to this.

Basil particularly relished the opportunity to engage with the discussion and analysis of empirical data. In discussing design issues he would raise all sorts of awkward questions, pushing for watertight sampling criteria and larger samples, scrutinizing interview schedules, probing for critical questions that might be asked about the integrity of the data. It was in the analysis of data that Basil became particularly engaged and inspired. From the smallest fragment of data he would set about the construction of categories, networks and relationships. These would not always hold up – the value of the enterprise was the exemplification of a process, a way of doing things, the development of the beginnings of a language. His mode of analysis and its outcomes clearly drew on his own conceptual language, but he always allowed space for the development of one's own analysis, not least because this would provide a foil for the further development of his own perspective and subsequently sharpened one's work. To get the best benefit from this it was important not to go under, to hold a position.

To the extent that Basil led by example, supervision was a form of apprenticeship. Whilst it was clear that the outcome would be a more thorough piece of research, precisely what one would gain was difficult to define beyond the ability to do research. From Basil's perspective this process produced researchers. Within a relationship ostensibly between colleagues, Basil was clearly the adept and the student or colleague the novice. The pedagogic mode was predominantly implicit. The transformations in the acquirer related both to competence and disposition. The criteria of evaluation lay firmly with the transmitter. Basil was true in practice to his relational understanding of pedagogy. Research was something that could not be taught in a segmental or curricularized manner. It was much more than the acquisition of a range of skills and techniques.

The process of becoming a researcher concerned much more than just the production of the work, of course. It clearly also concerned positioning in one's chosen field and at least some attendance to what Basil called 'fieldwork', for him a necessary evil, which clearly he both enjoyed and was irritated by. Basil would initiate often lengthy discussions of the current state of sociology and of sociology of education, including somewhat personal discussion of key players in the field (or rather, for Basil, people who thought they were key players). One frequently used term of abuse was to identify someone as a scholar. For Basil, spending time in the library was to be minimized, an alibi for lack of thinking. His advice on the length of time needed to conduct a literature review would vary between two weeks and two days. At a meeting of supervisors someone once raised the issue that people who had retired (as Basil had at that point) had perhaps lost touch with the field. Basil's response to this was to declare 'my dear, I am the field'.

For Basil, the emphasis in research should be placed on the production of a language of description. This requires both conceptual and empirical imagination. It entails detailed engagement with data and the production of explicit principles of analysis, which enables others to engage with and challenge one's descriptions. The construction of a language to translate the language of enactment, our interviews, our documents and our field notes, into terms that are theoretically recognizable, for Basil, opened a space for both academic critique and for the voice of the researched to be heard. This was his response to the weak powers of description of social theory and provided a basis for a challenge to conformity to the dominant specialized languages of sociology. He had high aspirations for his research students.

Working with Basil was an intense experience. There were highs and lows, ups and downs. Basil was passionate and committed, and consequently at times angry and dismissive. In this context, and in others, if you did not have a troubled relationship with Basil you probably did not have a relationship at all. The aim of the exercise was to develop a robust voice of one's own but the stakes were high. They had to be because what you were doing was important to Basil, no matter how many games were played in the process, ultimately the work mattered. In my experience, Basil would not let disputes interfere with his obligations and commitment to supervision. In our one serious falling out we spent an hour and a half discussing the analysis of some of my interview transcripts, half an hour of him regaling me on how one of my recent publications was morally reprehensible (with copious examples) and then, of course, lunch. Any tensions had to be viewed in relation to a deep commitment in to the project in hand, the productivity of engagement and the need to spend time to get it right.

When the time did come for me to complete my PhD, Basil had a number of techniques to employ. These included offering to write sections himself and setting up unfavourable comparisons with the progress of other students. As an adept tactician he was well able to take advantage of circumstances and I offer you one example. For a number of months, whenever I thought things were going well, Basil would say how badly it was going and when I felt things were not so good, he would say how well he thought the work was progressing. I had just completed three or four chapters and was pleased with my progress. Early in December I went across to Basil's tiny room in Woburn Square with some work for him to read. Just after I sat down he declared that he was firmly of the opinion that I would never complete the thesis. I protested, stating that I felt that everything was in place and that I was really getting down to writing. No, he insisted, it had been going on for too long and he just could not see it happening. Rashly, I said that it would be done, in fact I would have the thesis completed by 6th January. He reached across the desk and took a piece of Institute headed paper. He wrote, 'Dear Peter, You will be glad to hear that Andrew Brown will complete his PhD thesis on 6th January. Yours, as ever, Basil'. He put the letter in an envelope and addressed it 'Peter Mortimore' (at that time Director of the Institute). The next week Basil showed me Peter's reply, in which he said how pleased he was to hear this excellent news. Thus began the worst Christmas break I have ever had. Thankfully, I did manage to get the remaining chapters written and in Basil's pigeon hole by 6th January (albeit with numerous notes marking sections to be completed). The thesis was submitted in March and examined in May.

Basil's academic and research concerns, many of which have been discussed today, clearly relate to the manner in which he worked as a supervisor. Whilst few of us have the chutzpah or the standing to adopt his pedagogic techniques, there is much that we can gain from his orientation to research and the challenging, enthralling and unique experience of having worked under his guidance. We should pay heed to the importance of having the highest expectations of students and of enabling them to resist classification and sub-ordination to dominant modes of theorizing and to develop a voice. Despite the pressures of the new research economy, we need to provide opportunities for the development of explicit and transparent languages of description and to allow the time and space to elaborate principles of analysis, particularly in the analysis of qualitative data. Underlying this there is the imperative for supervisors to exemplify good research practice and maintain a vibrant synergy between our teaching and research. Thank you Basil for this, and for so much more.

ELABORATING BERNSTEIN

The great sociologist and his pedagogic devices

Fred Inglis, Professor of Cultural Studies,
University of Sheffield

THE DEATH OF Basil Bernstein is a moment to take stock. He shot into prominence as though fired from below the stage with those first, astonishing papers introducing teachers to what became the slogans of restricted and elaborated codes. He came from the battlefield of working-class education himself, and had had his hurts before. Demobilized from bomb-aiming in Sunderland flying boats above the West African coast, a job in which he learned lots about verbal condensation and redundancy in the imperative tense, he joined the staff of the Bernard Baron Settlement in Stepney in order to persuade recalcitrant East Enders aged between 9 and 18 the necessity of keeping quiet, writing English, adding and subtracting, and take a spot of exercise.

He had left school at 14. He had an RAF education. He knew from both sides of the desk what he himself called the 'baffling and desperate' predicament of the teacher in inner-city schools. And like all teachers in that deep hole, he grappled with the gross discrepancy in interest shown by his pupils in English, arithmetic and civics as opposed to their absorption in classes on car maintenance, where his own concern was to get by without exposing too much his own terrific ignorance.

This was the price of experience. It costs, William Blake tells us, all that a man hath: his house, his wife, his children. Bernstein paid for the experience in the coin of grand theory. It is not a currency much handled by teachers in Britain, although his countless admirers worldwide – in Spain, Chile, Greece, Japan – spend it greedily with his features on the coinage. Here at home it was devalued in passionate, futile debate as to whether 'elaborated' meant just talking posh and 'restricted' meant ineducable.

Bernstein turned malice and misunderstanding, the cold bloody-mindedness of English academic competition, into grand theory as well. He rode the long swell of public debate about education with the heavy Victorian engineering at the heart of its hydraulics. At its crest, let us say in 1970, the just-arrived Secretary of State had ratified the long revolution which brought in comprehensive education, the generous-hearted Newsom report was still a sacred book, teachers were bachelors and masters of their own university degrees, the Schools Council was enjoined to knit together policy and intellectual life, the Houghton pay settlement was on the horizon.

By the end of Basil Bernstein's life last September, a moment at which he was, amazingly, still attaching new essays to the revised edition of that powerful work *Pedagogy, Symbolic Control and Identity*, the Schools Council was long gone, research was a despised word, the pay was spent, the nominal Secretary of State, David read-my-lips Blunkett was accusing teachers, as he ineffably put it, of 'an anything goes philosophy' and the just-in-time-resigned Chief Inspector had spent almost six years in publicly contemptuous and insolent derogation of teachers once his comrades, his students and, indeed, his intimates.

Over these years and out of these circlings of the Wheel of Fire, Basil Bernstein contrived a purity of diction and a grandly inclusive frame of explanation which offered to those who understood it naught for their comfort except the austere consolations of theoretic enlightenment.

Social class misunderstanding; the incommensurability of my speech and yours; the energy of relevance; the poetics of silence; the contradiction between the near and the far; the twistpoint of his mighty oeuvre is where these grand, elusive topics cross. They name, moreover, the besetting troubles of the pedagogue's existence. But we are all of us now pedagogues, now the baffled and desperate student-creatures of contemporary turbo-capitalism.

Starting with those 9-year-olds in 1958 as they chattered about the little pictures in front of them and explained what they could see of context and abstraction, Bernstein constructed almost single-handedly a classical sociology adequate to the headlong juggernaut, the creativity and destructiveness, of what we have come to call the Information Society. Classical sociology, as Durkheim and Weber taught him and us, reveals, to its contemporaries and for a little time after, those systems of general knowledge won out of particular inquisitiveness together with the codes of their communication. Bernstein fashioned for himself the twin instruments of 'classification' and 'framing' in order to reach for the central mystery of modern society, the ordering and management of ignorance and status.

In doing so, he illuminated for the first time the generator of passions and the engines of action. What we know quickens the little flame of self-belief and the desires it warms; how we learn it shapes our initiative and our obedience.

He taught these lessons hard: hard–difficult and hard–unyielding. He taught them rapidly, deploying the fearsome abstractions of his algebra with painful fluency, the palm of one hand flickering now up, now down, in time with the swift design of his social geometry. He was, as all great teachers must be, sometimes very frightening. You dared not disclose your incomprehension, still less ask him to slow down; you feared his scorn at your stupidity; you avoided his immediate demolition of your dim objections.

He took opposition completely to heart, never more so than when misunderstood. Indeed he wrote misprision into the heart of his theory, showing us how his enemies mistook him for their own, paltry advantage, responding, in one marvellous example, to a critique of his abstraction by taking us deep into the social meanings of the lavatory. Such self-defence was never self-regarding. It was undertaken in the name of theory-refinement; of enlightenment: of good old truth.

For misunderstanding and stupidity, the vagaries of the powerful and the demands of technicism were alike components of 'the pedagogic device', the black box at the heart of all our linguistic and symbolic transactions which he was the first to unlock and dismantle.

This is his bequest. It is a key to many mythologies. Armed with the dialectic of classification and framing, reading his map of knowledge in order to determine which bits of what we know are hierarchical and which horizontal, checking our chat for its segmental (or practical) as opposed to its horizontal (or theoretic) position, we open up the pedagogic device and find out what it does to make us what we are and what in turn we do to make it what it is.

We discover the making of our identity. The roles of allocation and suppression come into inexorable play, of change in context, of criteria for evaluation (by your superiors or by you yourself), and the brutal rules regulating what it all costs in time and money. As we heed the rules and rulers and take their orders, we bend and twist and distort them to our own, other ends until, at another end, the rules themselves are changed utterly, even while the rulers insist they are not.

Now, I hope, this valediction takes on a heroic strain. This famous man I am so praising fulfils the epic role not just of great sociologist (enough for most of us) but of leading intellectual. His context, chosen or not, is that of *opposition*. He shows us the limits of our imagination, and to do so, as Marx told us, is to move them.

In a late and rousing essay given, appropriately, at the University of the Aegean, Basil Bernstein turns the beam of this theory, as he was now entitled to do, upon the dominant meaning of our civilization, and finds it to be money. This is true, he claims and I applaud, as never before, and the devilish device is now regularly adjusted by the powerful so to dislocate identity and detach knowledge from the inwardness we think of (quite rightly) as our hearts and souls that we will do anything it directs us to do so long as it makes money.

'The principles of the market', he said, within earshot of the ghosts of the Stoics and Socratics, 'and its mangers are more and more the managers of the policy and practices of education.' Market relevance is the measure of management and the criterion of intellectual usefulness. Measurable results and mere productivity become, in the loathsome jargon of the day, performance indicators; what a hellish performance this *danse macabre* has turned into.

In these circumstances, he went on, 'knowledge is not like money, it *is* money' – after a thousand years of the Western curriculum, the intellectual forms inherited from trivium and quadrivium, 'knowledge is divorced from inwardness and literally dehumanised'. This is the incarnation of technisim.

No one can say it all happened unintentionally. Prime Minister, Secretary of State, HMCI and Andrew Adonis, the Richelieu of the whole ghastly business, know exactly what they do. They are midwives in Britain of impending transcontinental consumer totalitarianism.

There has, however, never been an effectively total totalitarianism. The victory of instrumental reason over faith, of 'outerness' over inwardness, of technique over morality, of order over transgression, is never complete and always resistible. Human incompetence, mindlessness and everyday awfulness are all dependably immortal. And it is Bernstein's genius to have shown us also the space of freedom alongside the iron cage of rationalization. When the voice of pedagogy relocates the message of thought a gap is opened up. When the device turns what-has-never-been-thought-before into what-everybody-thinks-now a great deal has to be allowed to escape and leak out. Thoughts are free spirits; the bars of the cage can't hold them in. It goes without saying that there is no freedom without a fight.

The genteel gaolers of modern incarceration do their damnedest to hold down and in freedom of thought in education. It can't be done.

It should be a source of enormous pride that such a thinker of the unthinkable as Basil Bernstein came from classrooms and remained within the study of education, so unfailingly treated by its parent academies with ignorant disdain. He has shown its practitioners and the teachers to whom they owe their solidarity how to think the unthinkable for themselves, where to find the room to do so, and – most important of all the lessons of dissent – how a critical theory will spontaneously generate opposition, engagement, insouciance, *fight*. The right and proper expression of our gratitude to him and of our duty to our students is to think such thoughts and teach others to think them for themselves.

FINAL REMARKS

*Julia Brannen, Professor in the Sociology
of the Family, Institute of Education,
University of London*

OUR REVELS NOW ARE ended – at least for the time being. However, it is clear that an amazing variety of activities is already under way to carry on this celebration of the life of Basil Bernstein and these will take forward his work and maintain his influence. In the longer term, the Institute is seeking ways of endowing a fund for a lecture series and scholarship in Basil's memory. In the shorter term, there are a number of other memorial celebrations, notably in Australia and Norway. There are to be conference symposia on Bernstein's work, for example in Britain and North America. There is to be a biennial conference devoted to research inspired by Bernstein's theory; the next is planned for 2002 and will take place in Cape Town. There are to be special issues of academic journals and internet forums and websites (www.ioe.ac.uk).

So, the time has now come to thank everyone who has taken part in this momentous occasion. On behalf of the Director, and particularly on behalf of Marion Bernstein and her family, I want to thank every one of you who has participated, in your different ways, in this celebration of Basil's life: all those who have come here today, Sir William Taylor who has guided us so gently through the morning's programme, those who have spoken and performed, and those who have worked so hard behind the scenes to make the event happen and the day run so smoothly – the conference office, the other support staff and the committee which has organized the proceedings. Thank you all for making this a very, very special occasion.

As this day has so clearly demonstrated, Bernstein has inspired several generations of researchers, students, educators and educationalists across the world. His legacy will be to continue to shape the way we do research and the way we understand the social world. Hopefully, it will stir us to find new

81

ways in which his remarkable theoretical insights can be brought to bear. I for one feel sure that Basil will be watching us and would want each of us to take heed of this maxim '*It is not thy duty to complete the work but neither art thou free to desist from it*'.[1] Not one of you is off the hook!

Back to work!

Note

1   Hebrew Ethics of the Future, Chapter 11, Verse 20.

PART TWO

LETTERS

LETTERS

University of Athens
Department of Early Childhood Education
13a Navarinou str.
106 80 Athens
Greece

To the Director of the Institute of Education, University of London

29 September 2000

We, the members of the General Assembly of the Department of Early Childhood Education, University of Athens, wish to express our sympathy for the loss of the world-distinguished thinker in Sociology of Education and Language, Basil Bernstein, Emeritus Professor of the University of London, as well as Honorary Doctorate of the University of Athens and the Department of Early Childhood Education in particular.

We will always remember him, and his powerful ideas will always be an inspiration to us.

Professor Anna Frangoudaki
Head of the Department of Early Childhood Education

From Lionel Elvin

I shall soon have retired from the Institute for 30 years and it is difficult to recall the work of one's colleagues in as much detail as one would wish. Basil Bernstein was an experienced research worker and one who, like Freud, put into circulation concepts that entered into the general stream of professional consciousness with beneficial effect. His distinction between restricted codes of language and wider codes, and his pleas that the former were 'languages' no less that the latter, was such a contribution. It was always not only profitable but a pleasure to talk with him about his work. He was indeed one of the chief ornaments of our Institute and a very pleasant man.

Office of the Schools Adjudicator
Vincent House
2 Woodland Road
Darlington
DL3 7PJ

To Professor G. Whitty
Institute of Education

18 January 2001

Dear Geoff

Like many others, I owe an intellectual debt to Basil. He provided new ways of looking at a whole range of issues which I and thousands of teachers and colleagues had to deal with, not as scholars, but as people working in and for school children in London and elsewhere. I also owe to Basil my presence at the Institute. He called on me unexpectedly one day when I was Secretary to the Association of County Councils – under-employed and overpaid, as I told him, wondering why he was there.

'Why not consider applying to the Institute?' was his immediate response. It was obvious he was poised for combat. Now, as you know, it was never easy to say anything other than 'yes, of course' to Basil. So that is just what I did.

He was such a restless intellect: rightly seeing that, whatever else it was required to become, the Institute must always remain a community of scholars. And scholars, he was clear, have rights – are not to be pushed about. So in retirement Basil was not always retiring. He retreated to what looked like a not particularly large cupboard in Woburn Square. At one point, his voice failed him and he found print insufficiently forceful to express his opinions on the way such an eminent emeritus professor was being treated. Photographs were plonked on my desk. There was Basil in a variety of poses: peering from behind a mass of loose documents; squeezing past a tiny desk toward a horrible chair that was all there was room for – all accompanied by expressions of extreme anguish.

Basil was never one to put up peaceably with the insolence of office. So he will be sadly missed and I hope some way can be found to provide, within the Institute, some permanent record of that irrepressible spirit to whom the Institute and Scholarship and many of us owe so much.

Yours

P.A. Newsam

Waseda University
School of Education
2-6-1 Nishi-Waseda
Shinjuku-ku
Tokyo, Japan

6 January 2001

To whom it may concern

For the memory of Professor B. Bernstein

We wish to express our deepest sympathy on the passing of Professor B. Bernstein.

Professor B. Bernstein was one of the greatest scholars that we have ever known. We will never forget his thoughtfulness and kindness.

I learned that there is to be a memorial ceremony for him at the Institute of Education, University of London. I feel fortunate to have met and talked to him in 1999 in London, when I visited there with the support of the British Council and the UK–Japan Education Forum. I have been able to advance my research very successfully thanks to his advice.

My supervisor, Shozan Shibano, Emeritus Professor at Kyoto University, has known Professor Bernstein since the 1960s. Please accept our deepest sympathy.

Mutsuko Tendo
School of Education

PART THREE

WRITTEN TRIBUTES

RECONTEXTUALIZING BASIL BERNSTEIN

Michael W. Apple, John Bascom
Professor of Curriculum and Institution and
Educational Policy Studies, University of Wisconsin,
Madison, USA

I WANT TO USE this brief statement to say some things that are both academic and personal. Let me begin with the academic. As someone from the United States, my initial experiences with Basil Bernstein's work were largely determined by the specific configuration of social and educational problems recognized as legitimate (at least by those in power) in the US. This set of problems did not map on in any exact way to those seen as crucial in the UK.

Thus, the writings of Bernstein that had made an impact in the United States were his early socio-linguistic work on class and codes. The idea of linguistic 'difference' seemed powerful to academics and policy makers in a nation that had been searching for unitary and one-dimensional cultural explanations that would explain why poor and especially Black children did poorly in school. Yet, his emphasis on class was largely dropped when it arrived on our shores. This is not surprising, since for a variety of reasons class discourse has historically played less of a powerful role here, something that the academy not only has not altered, but has itself reproduced. Instead, Bernstein's work was transmuted into the already widespread discourse of the 'culture of poverty', which itself was then connected to race, given the historic association of race and poverty in the popular consciousness in the US. To all too many scholars and policy makers, 'we' now had an even more subtle explanation of poor Black achievement in schools. 'They' were flawed language users who used flawed language. This explanation cohered with decades, indeed centuries, of research – some of it deeply flawed both empirically and conceptually, to say nothing of its racist tendencies – that had either set out to prove Black inferiority or had come to that conclusion 'reluctantly' due to the supposed weight of its data. Today, we would associate this with the manner in which the politics of whiteness works in subtle and not so subtle ways.

But, of course, in an appreciative statement about Basil Bernstein, it is also important to recognize that the entire case of the US appropriation of a very limited aspect of his work is also a fascinating example of what Bernstein would recognize as an instance of recontextualization. Basil became an example of his own theoretical interventions. Pulled out of its originating context, and reappropriated into a set of specific historical struggles and debates, its meaning was redefined by a new set of rules. In words taken from his essay 'On pedagogic discourse', the text 'undergoes a transformation prior to its relocation [in a new context]'. As the text is 'delocated' from its original location and 'relocated' into a new situation, the logic and power relations of the recontextualizing agents in the new location ensure that 'the text is no longer the same text'. In this kind of situation, not only does the meaning of a text change, but so does its *use*. Thus, Basil's analyses were then taken up and employed by recontextualizing agents within the state and the academy in the United States to support policies whose effects he had critically discussed in his work on the sociology of curriculum that had accompanied his socio-linguistic research. I often wonder if this instance of Bernstein himself being subject to delocation and relocation might not have been one of the motivations for his later theoretical investigations into the problem of recontextualization. It is worth exploring.

While some of his socio-linguistic writings were visible here, the work that accompanied it was invisible. Thus, all of the significant essays included in, say, *Class, Codes, and Control Volume 3* were basically unknown. In large part that had to do with the empirical traditions that dominated sociology of education in the US – status attainment, social stratification, and similar orientations – and with the apolitical and atheoretical impulses that guided such work. Further, within sociology of education, by and large the complex issues surrounding the relationship between knowledge and power had little tradition. These issues instead were found in critical curriculum studies. Thus, in the early 1970s when I began to publish the material that ultimately led to *Ideology and Curriculum*, there was almost no history of such work in the sociology of education in the United States. When I first read Bernstein's essays that ultimately went into *Class, Codes, and Control Volume 3*, it was as if I had discovered an entire branch of my own family that I had not known existed. Even before I met him and had become a colleague and a friend, Bernstein became one of my most important teachers.

This does not mean we agreed on everything of importance. Indeed, we often had serious disagreements in print and in personal conversations. Yet the very existence of such disagreements is worth noting. Only the positions of those for whom one has a good deal of respect are even worth disagreeing with. The fact that, even with these disagreements, he is one of those on whose shoulders I and so many others stand, speaks to the respect he earned. Of course, I am wrong to put this in the past tense. His work has a truly lasting value, a point made crystal clear to me when my own students – and their students – continue to be profoundly influenced by Basil Bernstein's writings.

I remember our first meeting in the mid-1970s. I had been invited to give a lecture at the Institute of Education and, to be honest, I was rather nervous. It was my first set of lectures in England – and Basil Bernstein was sitting directly in front of me as I spoke. After my lecture, Basil came up to me and began discussing, in detail and in his own engaging way, where he agreed and disagreed with my analysis of the relationship between curriculum and power. He invited me for dinner, a dinner that lasted for hours and hours. We 'played' intellectually. We argued. (He did not take lightly to sycophants.) And then we argued some more. He drew diagrams on paper napkin after paper napkin, until we had to take some from another table. I trace some of the ways I ask certain questions about the dialectical relationships among culture, economy, and the state from that evening – and from many evenings that followed over the years. But it would be wrong to mention only the academic here. Basil's repeated letters of support when my older son was seriously ill remind me of the complicated man behind the pen as well.

The Jewish theologian and political activist Abraham Heschel once said that to be human is to 'wrestle' with uncertainty. Wrestling with my agreements and disagreements with Bernstein became a continuing process over the years. Knowing him changed me. What more can one ask of a teacher?

BASIL BERNSTEIN

*Julia Brannen, Professor in the Sociology of the
Family, Institute of Education, University of London*

THE DEATH OF Basil Bernstein on 24 September 2000 constitutes an immeasurable public as well as a profound private loss. Basil's contribution to British social science research has been, and continues to be, highly significant. This is evident in the expanding critical mass of scholars throughout the world who take inspiration from him and seek to apply his body of theory to their research.

In this short piece I want to pay tribute to Basil, and in particular to his commitment to methodology. In the 1980s and 1990s as a contract researcher at Thomas Coram Research Unit, I came under Basil's spell. Not being a sociologist of education, I had never studied Bernstein's work formally. Moreover, in directly communicating his ideas, Basil would insist I need only read his work selectively. Whatever my intellectual or research problem, Basil was always ready and willing to apply his imaginative and rigorous mind to it. It was sheer delight to listen to and talk with him and, when in the mid-1990s we found ourselves co-editing a collection of essays, mostly written by psychologists, to honour our close colleague, Barbara Tizard, this proved an enormously enriching experience (Bernstein and Brannen 1996.) Above all, I shall remember Basil for his conversations: Basil's ability to engage in the discussion of ideas and their formulation and, in the moment of their realization, to make it such fun! If this was a process of teaching and learning, which it clearly was, then the great art of the teacher and the magic of the learning that went on lay in the fact that neither of us noticed it or even cared! With Basil's death has come the slow realization that I will have to make do with his books, which, for the time being at least, seem poor substitutes!

Basil gave methodology a central place in research. He was a most enthusiastic supporter when in the mid-1990s, I helped to found a new methodology journal – the *International Journal of Social Research Methodology:*

Theory and Practice. For the journal, Basil's death is a double loss since he was a founding member of its editorial board and wrote an article for the journal which, sadly, was not published in his lifetime.

Basil regarded methodology as an intrinsic part of the processes of conceptualization and theoretical development, as his work makes so abundantly clear. A fierce advocate of rigour in social science research, Basil viewed with concern the growing marketization of research. Within the new research funding economy, Basil saw it as all the more important to champion this cause in the context of the increasing time pressures and production demands placed upon researchers and research students. In this context, he identified and problematized the central features of research: research as a culture, research as a craft, and research as a material condition.

Research is a culture which involves mechanisms of enculturation; researchers are required to learn the rules that govern the mores and practices of researchers as a cultural group. In terms of Basil's own theory, researchers must learn to recognize the languages of the researcher group and must learn to speak those languages. In carrying out their own empirically-based studies, researchers are required also to learn the language of their informants and to translate between the languages of the researcher group (the relevant conceptual languages) and the languages of research participants (Bernstein 2000). Basil feared that the new funding conditions were undermining the processes of researcher enculturation. He feared that the growth in emphasis on short-term training courses and on shorter completion rates would supplant the longer-term process by which students learn to do research. He saw a danger that training courses would provide 'quick fixes', 'technological choices', and 'routinised procedures' which would displace 'theoretical innovation and methodological disturbance' (Bernstein 2000: 32).

Basil believed that research is essentially a craft that requires each of us to serve an apprenticeship. PhDs should not be regarded as 'driving licences' but as 'licences to explore' (2000: 32). As a supervisor of research students, stories are legion about Basil's commitment to his students: the generosity with which he gave vast amounts of his time not only to reading but also to discussing his students' work. Even more abundant are the reports of his generosity in offering his own theoretical insights and frameworks for the students to make their own. For Basil, research was essentially a practice to be learned by doing. He was a trusty companion to students on their tortuous journeys of exploration, if unsettling in the searching questions he always posed.

Basil was also keenly conscious of the material context and conditions under which mainly contract researchers carry out research. For at the heart of his own theory of the transformation of knowledge into pedagogic communication, Basil was concerned with social structure. As Pro-Director of Research within the Institute of Education for some years in the 1980s, Basil spear-headed an organization through which contract researchers might strengthen their then weak and lowly position within academe and might redress some of the constraining aspects of what he termed the researcher 'culture of impermanence'.

Basil's theory always seemed to me germane to understanding the wider contemporary world beyond the orthodox boundaries of education. It offers enormous potential and the article he wrote for the *International Journal of Social Research Methodology* (Bernstein 2001) is just one example of this. The theoretical distinctions it proposes with respect to social class have enormous currency in today's rapidly changing world of work. They pose considerable challenges to those of us who continue to view social class as a central mechanism for the distribution of resources, yet too often cling to routinized definitions.

As the Memorial Celebration and the very many tributes paid by colleagues testify, as a person and through his work, Basil has made an indelible mark upon us. But he would not have wished that such appreciations of his contribution to social science to be valedictory. Rather, he would have wanted his work to inspire current and future generations of researchers and research students to carry on the endeavour and to find new ways in which his remarkable theoretical insights can be brought to bear under rigorous methodological conditions. It is to be hoped that researchers will continue to take up the challenge and carry on this important work. *'It is not thy duty to complete the work but neither art thou free to desist from it'* (Hebrew Ethics of the Future, Chapter 11 verse 20).

References

Bernstein, B. (2000) *Pedagogy, Symbolic Control and Identity: Theory, research, critique*. Lanham, MD: Rowman and Littlefield.

Bernstein, B. (2001) 'Symbolic control: issues of empirical description of agencies and agents', *'International Journal of Social Research Methodology* 4 (1), January.

Bernstein, B. and Brannen, J. (1996) *Children, Research and Policy*. London: Taylor and Francis.

REMEMBERING BASIL BERNSTEIN

Aaron V. Cicourel, Research Professor,
Department of Cognitive Science, and
Hugh Mehan, Professor of Sociology,
both at University of California, San Diego, USA

IN THE SUMMER OF 1968, while we both attended a conference at Berkeley organized by Dan Slobin, John Gumperz and Susan Ervin-Tripp on language acquisition across cultures, Basil presented a lecture on restricted and elaborated speech registers. We began to correspond in the early 1960s and the first author spent the academic year 1970–1 with Basil at the Institute of Education. The original work was exciting because it linked the idea of language use to what has been long perceived in Britain (and elsewhere) as class bias in education, a bias that tacitly if not explicitly assumed that there was a clear correspondence or a least a correlation between language use and a person's general intellectual capabilities. Basil's notion of elaborated and restricted codes, however, neither implicitly nor explicitly made this assumption but many readers of his work made such a connection because the notion was adopted by Karl Bereiter and Siegfrid Englemann in the United States (see below). The fact that tests of intellectual capabilities are often biased in terms of a knowledge and the use of standard language (English in the present case) can be found in all areas of the world where English is spoken.

As is often the case in the social sciences, Basil's own experiences influenced his research. For example, being born into a part of London where a particular vernacular was spoken, provided him with first-hand knowledge of how differences in language use had nontrivial consequences for the way a person was perceived, accepted, treated indifferently or ignored. The problems associated with language became a source of frequent discussion because one of us was doing research among a low-income deaf group in South London.

The criticisms of some of Basil's early work did not always respect his broad theoretical knowledge of sociology and language use in everyday life, especially in educational activities. We remember a small, informal seminar of Michael Halliday's at University College during the 1970–1 academic year in which many of the ideas expressed therein could be found in 'Systematic functional linguistics'. Ruqaiya Hasan was affiliated with Basil's group at the time. Basil was an important contributor to the seminar discussions and he was keenly aware of the hiatus between attempts to link language use to abstract theoretical notions in stratification and educational research.

Basil perhaps has been misunderstood and under-appreciated in the United States because his work was implicated in the debates over language use that raged between Bill Labov and Karl Bereiter and Siegfried Englemann in the late 1960s and mid-1970s. Bereiter and Englemann (1966) referred to Basil's distinction between restricted and elaborated codes to help explain the poor academic performance of low-income and ethnic-minority youth in urban US schools. They concluded that the language and thought of low-income, mostly black youth was inadequate for complex expression. Labov's (1972) strong attack of the notion of 'deficit thinking' in Bereiter and Engelmann's work by extension included Basil's theorizing. Black English Vernacular (BEV) was rule-governed, logical, and grammatical, Labov countered, but conformed to grammatical rules that were somewhat distinct from so-called 'standard English'. By failing to take the power-laden dimensions of testing situations into account, and by confusing deep and surface structures of speech, Labov said Bereiter, Englemann, and Bernstein had overlooked the richness and complexity of the speech of low-income youth in US cities.

We underscore the importance of Bernstein's early work because there has been considerable controversy over its interpretation and methodological and empirical exploration. We had discussed some of our misgivings with Basil and feel that, in some respects, he could have done more to clarify some of the misunderstanding that clouded his subsequent, serious theoretical contributions, for example his work on social stratification and his theory of pedagogy. Such concepts as 'recontextualization', strong (or one-sided) and weak (or shared) control or 'framing', and 'classification' have been referenced widely beyond the study of educational theory and practice.

We do not think Basil meant to characterize the speech of low-income youth as illogical, ungrammatical or deficient and thereby blame these victims for their lowly position in the social order. People who draw this conclusion do not understand the deeper meaning of his work. The body of his work that spanned more than 40 years can be better understood in the context of theories seeking to explain the social and cultural reproduction of social inequality.

In its most economically deterministic form (Bowles and Gintis 1976) 'reproduction theory' emphasizes the similarity between the social relations of production in the workplace and the personal interaction between teachers and students in the classroom. The relationship of authority and control among educators and students replicates the authority and control among supervisors and workers. This 'correspondence', for example, can be seen in students' lack of control over what is taught to them and the workers' lack of control over the content, pacing and timing of their work, as well as the role of grades and the role of wages as external or extrinsic rewards. By calling attention to the 'correspondence' between the structure of schooling and the structure of work, Bowles and Gintis shifted attention away from the naive functionalist orientation that posited success as a matter of individual hard work and effort. But the rigid structural correspondence that Bowles and Gintis posit between the educational and economic systems does not reveal the social processes of social reproduction.

Much more than Bowles and Gintis, Bernstein (and Bourdieu) give serious attention to the interactional dimension of social life and treat the cultural sphere as an object of critical inquiry in its own right – not just as an appendage to the economic sphere. We agree with MacLeod's assessment of Basil's work: 'Through his theory of language codification and its relationship to social class on the one hand and schooling on the other, Bernstein links micro- and macro-sociological issues' (1987: 15).

Basil has left us with an enviable legacy of serious scholarship that goes beyond theory as a kind of cottage industry. Unlike most sociological theorists, Basil was constantly involved in the countless research projects of his many students and was intimately aware of the necessity of linking theory to research and then to additional theory that would lead to further research. We will miss his serious scholarship, penetrating insights, and wonderful (though sometimes scathing) wit.

References

Bereiter, K. and Englemann, S. (1966) *Teaching the Disadvantaged Child in the Preschool*. Englewood Cliffs, NJ: Prentice Hall.

Bowles, S. and Gintis, H.I. (1976) *Schooling in Capitalist America*. New York: Basic Books.

Halliday, A.K. (1976) 'Systematic functional linguistics'. In G.R. Kress (ed.) *System and Function in Language*. Oxford: Oxford University Press.

Labov, W. (1972) *Language in the Inner City*. Philadelphia: University of Pennsylvania Press.

MacLeod, J. (1987) *Ain't No Makin It: Leveled aspirations in a low-income neighborhood*. Boulder, CO: Westview Press.

BERNSTEIN AND VYGOTSKY

Researching socio-institutional effects in socio-cultural theory

Harry Daniels, Professor of Special Education and Educational Psychology, University of Birmingham

MANY THEORETICAL accounts of the socio-genesis of individual consciousness refer to the work of the Russian psychologist and semiotician L.S. Vygotsky. Most of these accounts lack a sociological perspective. Bernstein's work offers many parallels and is also of real value in that it suggests that when we try to understand why people act in particular ways we should study thinking, feeling and communication in the context of specific forms of institutional organization and practice. The emphasis on institutions that is foregrounded in Bernstein's work is almost absent in Vygotsky.

Wertsch (1985) suggests that Vygotsky's theoretical work can be understood in terms of a reliance on a developmental method; the claim that higher mental functioning in the individual has its origins in social life; the claim that a full account of human mental functioning must be based on an understanding of the way in which psychological tools and signs act in the mediation of social factors. Here psychological tools are those symbolic artefacts – signs, symbols, texts, formulae, graphic-symbolic devices – that help individuals master their own 'natural' psychological functions such as perception, memory, attention (Kozulin 1998: 1).

Within this theoretical framework there is a requirement for a structural description of social settings which provides principles for distinguishing between social practices. Descriptions of this sort would be an important part of the apparatus required to carry out empirical investigation and analysis of the psychological consequences for individuals of different forms of social organization. However, description itself would not be enough. Vygotsky's writing on the way in which psychological tools and signs act in the mediation of social factors does not engage with a theoretical account of the appropriation and/or and production of psychological tools within specific forms of activity within or across institutions.

Bernstein seeks to link semiotic tools with the structure of material activity. Crucially he draws attention to the processes that regulate the structure of the tool rather than just its function.

> Once attention is given to the regulation of the structure of pedagogic discourse, the social relations of its production and the various modes of its recontextualising as a practice, then perhaps we may be a little nearer to understanding the Vygotskian tool as a social and historical construction.
>
> (Bernstein 1993: xx)

He also argues that much of the work that has followed in the wake of Vygotsky 'does not include in its description how the discourse itself is constituted and recontextualised'.

> The socio-historical level of the theory is, in fact, the history of the biases of the culture with respect to its production, reproduction, modes of acquisition and their social relations.   (Bernstein 1993: xviii)

In Engestrom's (1996) work within Activity Theory the production of the outcome is discussed but not the production and structure of the tool itself.

As Ratner (1997) notes, Vygotsky did not consider the ways in which concrete social systems bear on psychological functions. He discussed the general importance of language and schooling for psychological functioning; however, he failed to examine the real social systems in which these activities occur and reflect. Vygotsky never indicated the social basis for this new use of words. His social analysis was thus reduced to a semiotic analysis that overlooked the real world of social praxis.

> The feature that can be viewed as the proximal cause of the maturation of concepts, is a specific way of using the word, specifically the functional application of the sign as a means of forming concepts.
>
> (Vygotsky 1987: 131)

Whilst it is quite possible to interpret 'a specific way of using the word' to be an exhortation to analyse the activities in which the word is used and meaning negotiated, this was not elaborated by Vygotsky himself. The analysis of the structure and function of semiotic psychological tools in specific activity contexts is not explored.

Thus the following issues may be regarded as points for development in contemporary post-Vygotskian theory and research:

- Insufficient empirical study of socio-institutional effects
- Tendency to under-theorize differences between schools in terms of institutional effects on the social formation of mind
- Lack of theory of structure of tool
- Lack of theory of constitution and recontextualization of the psychological tool

Bernstein's (1996) book outlined a model for understanding the construction of pedagogic discourse. In this context pedagogic discourse is a source of psychological tools.

> The basic idea was to view this (pedagogic) discourse as arising out of the action of a group of specialised agents operating in specialised setting in terms of the interests, often competing interests of this setting.
>
> (Bernstein 1996: 116)

The distribution of power and principles of control differently specialize structural features and their pedagogic communicative relays.

Bernstein's (1996) book also provides a discussion of the distinction between instructional and regulative discourse. The former refers to the transmission of skills and their relation to each other, and the latter refers to the principles of social order, relation and identity. Whereas the principles and distinctive features of instructional discourse and its practice are relatively clear (the what and how of the specific skills/competences to be acquired and their relation to each other), the principles and distinctive features of the transmission of the regulative are less clear as this discourse is transmitted through various media and may indeed be characterized as a diffuse transmission. Regulative discourse communicates the school's (or any institution's) public moral practice, values beliefs and attitudes, principles of conduct, character and manner. It also transmits features of the school's local history, local tradition and community relations. Pedagogic discourse is modelled as one discourse created by the embedding of instructional and regulative discourse. This model of pedagogic discourse provides a response to one of the many theoretical demands which have remained unfulfilled in the post-Vygotskian framework. The rejection of the cognitive/affective dualism which Vygotsky announced was not followed by a model within which a unitary conception of thinking and feeling could be discussed and implemented within empirical research.

The language that Bernstein has developed allows researchers to take measures of school modality. That is to describe and position the discursive, organizational and interactional practice of the institution. Research may then seek to investigate the connections between the rules the children use to make sense of their pedagogic world and the modality of that world.

In one of his last journal papers, Bernstein (1999) moved his analysis to the internal principles of the construction and social base of pedagogic discourses. Having provided a theory of the construction of pedagogic discourse he moved to an analysis of the discourses subject to pedagogic transformation. This move will be of particular significance when this body of theory and its language of description is brought to bear on the discussion of the relationship between everyday and scientific concepts as outlined in *Thinking and Speech* (Vygotsky 1987). The analysis outlined by Bernstein (1999) allows for greater differentiation within and between the forms identified by Vygotsky. The analytical power of the distinctions made between vertical and horizontal discourses and hierarchical and horizontal knowledge structures provides research with an enhanced capacity to provide descriptions that capture the delicacy of the forms and their interrelation. This paper sets an important agenda for work in the future.

Bernstein provides an account of cultural transmission which is avowedly sociological in its conception. In turn the psychological account that has developed in the wake of Vygotsky's writing offers a model of aspects of the social formation of mind which is underdeveloped in Bernstein's work. Taken together these theoretical positions constitute important psychological tools in the development of theoretical and empirical work.

References

Bernstein, B. (1993) 'Foreword'. In H. Daniels (ed.) *Charting the Agenda: Educational activity after Vygotsky*. London: Routledge.

Bernstein, B. (1996) *Pedagogy, Symbolic Control and Identity: Theory, research, critique*. London: Taylor and Francis.

Bernstein, B. (1999) 'Vertical and horizontal discourse: an essay', *British Journal of Sociology of Education* 20 (2): 157–74.

Engestrom, Y. (1996) *Perspectives on Activity Theory*. Cambridge: Cambridge University Press.

Kozulin, A. (1998) *Psychological Tools: A sociocultural approach to education*. London: Harvard University Press.

Ratner, C. (1997) *Cultural Psychology and Qualitative Methodology: Theoretical and empirical considerations*. London: Plenum Press.

Vygotsky, L.S. (1987) *The Collected Works of L.S. Vygotsky. Vol. 1: Problems of General Psychology*. Including *Thinking and Speech*. (Edited by R.W. Rieber and A.S. Carton; translated by N. Minick.) New York: Plenum Press.

Wertsch, J. (1985) *Vygotsky and the Social Formation of Mind*. Cambridge, MA: Harvard University Press.

BASIL BERNSTEIN[1]

Sara Delamont, Reader in Sociology,
Cardiff University

BERNSTEIN hated retrospective analyses of his work, and flattering accounts of ideas 30 years old. He wanted us to engage with his current thinking. In this piece I have done that. Paul Atkinson (1985) has dealt with his work and his influence from the earliest papers to the mature books. After his retirement from the London Institute of Education in 1990 he became more productive than he had been in the previous decade while he was being honoured more overseas than in the UK. In the mid-1990s two *festschriften* were prepared for him. Alan Sadovnik (1995) edited a book in which the contributors looked back over Bernstein's work, and he then commented on these analyses. Sadovnik's long introductory essay to that volume covers Bernstein's work from 1984–1990. In Cardiff Paul Atkinson, Brian Davies and I (1995) took a contrasting approach. We commissioned people to look ahead: to explore how their own intellectual projects were developing from Basil Bernstein's work. We kept our *festschrift* a secret from Professor Bernstein until it was at the publishers so he could not interfere with us or our contributors. He liked some of the papers and hated others. Commentating on his work, even favourably, was always to risk his displeasure. The Cardiff volume was launched with a short invitational conference, the two *festschriften* were celebrated at AERA in New York in 1996. A ballroom was full of people who wanted to hear Bernstein and he gave one of his spellbinding performances there. The audience included some of the most famous sociologists of education in the USA: his life and work were properly applauded. I am glad that the two books, and the two events, were organized while Basil Bernstein was well enough to be part of them.

Basil Bernstein was a Durkheimian, but a French Durkheimian like Mauss and Levi-Strauss, not an Anglo-Saxon Durkheimian like Radcliffe Brown and Talcott Parsons. His concerns were closer to Bourdieu's than to Halsey's or

Coleman's: he did not 'fit' sociology of education, but was too closely associated with that sub-specialism to be properly appreciated for the far-reaching scope of his ideas on class, inequality, gender and the labour market.

The last letter I had from him was his reaction to my article in the Millennial issue of *Sociology* (Delamont 2000). He wrote, in shaky handwriting:

A very brave paper. I enjoyed the structure as much as the content.

He then went on to produce a precise, and incisive, analysis of the central contention of my paper:

It is possible that anxieties sociologists increasingly have about their own status makes them distance themselves from university pariah discourses like education. Sociologists of Education are institutionally marginalised: very few in departments of sociology, ghettoised in pariah sites. Further our kin regard us a hybrid, as many do not hold first degrees in sociology or second from 'reputable' examplars of the subject. We are not kosher and live in profane places.

Only a foolhardy commentator would try to improve on that verdict: certainly all those of us who work in the sociology of education know we do indeed live in profane places.

Note
1 This piece previously appeared in Network, the newsletter of the British Sociological Association.

References
Atkinson, P.A. (1985) *Language, Structure and Reproduction*. London: Methuen.
Atkinson, P.A., Davies, W.B. and Delamont, S. (eds) (1995) *Discourse and Reproduction*. Cresskill, N.J.: Hampton.
Delamont, S. (2000) 'The anomalous beasts', *Sociology* 34 (1): 95–112.
Sadovnik, A. (ed.) (1995) *Knowledge and Pedagogy*. Norwood, N.J.: Ablex.

THE IMPORTANCE OF BASIL BERNSTEIN

Mario Dias, former Professor of Sociology of Education,
Universidad del Valle, Cali, Colombia

I ALWAYS REMEMBER a gift a friend of mine gave me when he returned to Colombia from London: volumes 1 and 3 of *Class, Codes and Control*. After reading them with great difficulty I took an important decision in my life: to know Bernstein and to study with him. From 1981 to 1984 I had the opportunity to relate with his thought, his sensibility and his humour. His initial rejection of my Foucauldian view of discourse and of pedagogic discourse was slowly transformed into an acceptance of my viewpoints and into a deep friendship which made it possible for me to discuss with him the post-structuralist positions. In his last seminar in the doctoral programme at Universidad del Valle in Cali, Colombia, he invited me to continue analysing the inside and the outside of the black box of pedagogic device: a difficult if not embarrassing task.

It is difficult to write about a man whose life project was a permanent confrontation, and more difficult when he contributed to open and deepen my understanding to most of the crucial problems of my own research. However, I consider that a great thinker, like a great book, is polyphonic. The voice of a great thinker always offers possibilities and impossibilities; his texts are open to difficulties, to the uncertainties of ambiguities. A great thinker moves in the boundaries of theoretical and biographical adventures. He celebrates weak classifications between vertical horizontal discourses. The voice of a great thinker is the signifier for multiple voices, voices that reproduce, oppose, distort, create and recreate. Bernstein was that type of thinker. His intellectual biography was full of new insights in which explanations, formulations and criticism were a complete personal attitude towards life: a new reading every day. He was aware that a thinker – not an author – can make mistakes.

For this reason, his texts were subjected to a permanent review and correction to the point that we could abstract from his work a sociology of criticism.

The importance of Bernstein for us – his intellectual project which is an integration of theory and life – was that of producing a new way for thinking of and making sociology from a synthesis of different semiotics: from the most traditional views to postmodern perspectives. If his attitude of mind was close to that of Durkheim he owes a debt to structuralism, post-structuralism, Marxism, and to all their realizations in theories and perspectives produced in modern social sciences.

Like Weber, he refused to describe himself as a sociologist. He preferred to call himself a boundary thinker, a thinker of social relations, a thinker of communication. He was aware that there is a semiotics of distortion in social communication. Around communication he formulated the same question for more than 40 years: 'Are there general principles underlying the transformation of knowledge into pedagogic communication?' In this respect he stated: 'when making the question I felt like moving in the obscurity'. And that obscurity, which in my view was more visible in the 1980s, was a part of his intrinsic objective: to make conscious and explicit the semiotic grammar underlying pedagogic communication. This is the challenge of our concerns with Bernstein's theory: how to continue his remarkable task of making clear the transformation of the social through symbolic means within and between individuals and groups.

I have been always interested in scrutinizing what I call 'the archaeology of his theory', built in the articulation of diversity, and remember his different kinds of answers to my permanent question about his intellectual and personal antecedents of his formulations. 'You can start at Kant, and go through Durkheim and Weber', he told me one day, ' but, in essence I am a Kantian'. If there is in this answer a clue to pedagogic discourse and its regulative basis, is then the archaeology of Bernstein's thought the recontextualizing of Kantian practical reason? I think Bernstein offers a remarkable contribution to the understanding of the emergence of the more diverse forms of morals and identities deployed in time and space. His Kantian sense, filtered through Durkheim and influenced by the most contradictory perspectives (Marxism, functionalism), produced his approach to the increased opposition between the internalization and the externalization of subjectivity and identity in regulative contexts.

If he took distance from the post-structuralist, and rejected definition as structuralist, he implicitly reflected or embedded in his writings the language and underlying notions from these perspectives. His recent texts implicitly summon up positions, influences and agreements and disagreements to post-structuralism, to the point that the final statement of his book *Pedagogy*,

Symbolic Control and Identity ('Oh dear, is this a structuralist analysis?') reflects his refusal to be positioned within a frame (Bernstein 1996). Was this a way to escape from the transitivity of determinism and the intransitivity of its realizations? Or was a way to show how the nature of mediation is the basic principle for production, reproduction and change, present in any kind of action, position and perspective?

Bernstein represented the language of the impossible; his life was a permanent grammar of imagination. He used to break the boundaries between imagination and the impossible. One of his last papers is an introduction to the inspiration of explanatory ideas about the collective forces that stimulate the postmodern 'totemic' society: symbolic modalities close to ritualistic identities which become particularistic emblematic languages that flow as disseminated generalized means to imagining the difference in the massive practice of consumption. His statement about the triumphant silence of the voice of pedagogic discourse in a totally pedagogized society is very symbolic. To what extent can the impossible escape from pedagogy can be considered a sociological law? The only way to escape is to die, but, as he told me in a meeting in Colombia, 'to die is the best way to be alive'.

Glory to his memory.

Reference
Bernstein, B. (1996) *Pedagogy, Symbolic Control and Identity: Theory, research, critique.* London: Taylor and Francis.

BASIL BERNSTEIN[1]

Mary Douglas, former Professor of Anthropology,
University College London

I MET BASIL BERNSTEIN in 1964 or early 1965. I had just handed in to the publisher the typescript of *Purity and Danger*. Then I read his short article, 'A socio-linguistic approach to social learning' in the *Penguin Survey of the Social Services*. It was electrifying. I had never read anything like it, I didn't understand it either, but I remember the sense of excitement. When I reread it now I can see his whole future programme clearly sketched in its pages. Here was a thinker engaged with the deepest problems about culture. In those days anthropology was expected to provide understanding of ourselves, but our calling was to do it by studying other people, not us: people living in remote savannahs, mountain fastnesses, or tropical islands. Bernstein was working on the same problems but in a framework that applied to us, ourselves, in modern industrial society. He summed up his main preoccupation as 'the transmission of culture'. His subject was truth, the relation of words to things, translation, interpretation/misinterpretation, all these questions placed in one grand perspective, the pre-selection of meaning. It was axiomatic for the anthropologists of those times that understanding must always come filtered through a screen of prejudice and social bias, in other words, the local culture, but we do not know how to apply the axiom to ourselves. The anthropologists who broke away from the mould and made distinguished fieldwork-based studies of us at home (factory workers, Durham coal miners, Marks and Spencer, shop keepers in Ireland, villages in Wales), aimed to present straight ethnography. They did not expect to find answers to philosophical questions about cognition, or the fundamental issue of how individuals become acculturated social beings.

Since the expansive days of the 1950s different established disciplines were each discovering that they had a social dimension that had hitherto been overlooked. By the 1960s a range of sub-disciplines was created to fill this gap; socio-linguistics was still fairly new, as were social geography, social anthropology, social psychology and communications. The learned disciplines treated the newly added social element as a decorative appendage to the main job. Bernstein had a famous caustic wit and he could be very funny about the marginalizing of so-called 'inter-disciplinary' studies. The 'socio' part of linguistics, psychology, geography, etc., was mainly taken as given, which meant taken from textbooks (or newspapers), anecdotal, not systematized or theorized. There was no expectation that sociology itself would need to be re-thought. It was nobody's job to turn sociology upside down and inside out, but this is what Bernstein was doing. No wonder his teaching was difficult to accept.

Basil Bernstein's central idea was that language is mediated by social relations. 'Humans speak', he would declare, 'but sociology is silent about it'. He might have added that language is produced in a social process, but linguists are silent about that too. At that time the link between humans and their speech acts was taken to lie within the individual psyche. To propose the social structure as the governing factor was revolutionary, and to many it was distasteful. For myself it was a shock to learn that the words I utter and the sentiments I express are called forth by the expectations of the people I live with. On Bernstein's theory everyone's speech responds to strong cultural pressures, not least those speakers who most pride themselves on autonomous thought. It was a theory of speech forms responding to two types of social control: one through positioning and one through individualizing.

The socio-linguistic analysis that Bernstein applied to two social classes, one fixed, one mobile, corresponded to family life of the two social classes described by Young and Wilmott in Bethnal Green[2] and Elizabeth Bott.[3] But he derived it initially not from study but from his own direct experience as a teacher in his first job. Here also arose his passionate interest in the sociology of education. He drew a contrast between social classes defined as middle (privileged, educated and expecting to be upwardly mobile), and working class (underprivileged, blue-collar, not highly educated, not expecting their children to transcend their lowly beginnings). All the theoretical emphasis was on the scope for mobility. The 'restricted speech codes' of working classes showed their recognition that they were stuck. The 'elaborated speech codes' of middle classes abetted their strenuous seeking for self-improvement. Whenever a ceiling on opportunity left speech unburdened by the need to explore and exploit new social environments he expected to find positioned family types. They would flourish, not only in deprived working classes, but also in privileged aristocratic or military families using respectively differing forms of the restricted code to speak to each other.

His examples of how the middle-class mother speaks to her child are hilariously funny, and not without malice. Her elaborated speech code responded to the sense that her first obligation was to teach her children to be able to articulate verbally in order to be able to negotiate their future. The kind of individualism she established in family life was well designed to respond to opportunities for social advancement. The middle classes who were preparing their children for a more dynamic future hoped they would be ready to move around, enter new educational establishments, keep starting again in new jobs, and so on. To this end they taught their children to be highly articulate, since they would have to be able to express themselves eloquently to the strangers who could help them in their social struggle.

The other type of family did not organize its internal social relations verbally but by enactment of formal patterns of roles in household space and time. They observed principled distinctions of gender and age, indoors and outdoors, and a structure of times. These positions did not need to be verbalized; they could be seen functioning. It was learning by doing. The girls and boys had different tasks for helping in the house; for seating at meals every place was patterned according to the same criteria; there were no negotiations for bedtimes; the age rule sent the younger children to bed first. In what he called 'positional families', there was no room for arguing about individual privileges and responsibilities. They were laid down in easily understood patterns of society. Speech did not have to carry the burden of argument about status and rights. So rhetorical skills were freed up for other uses, such as creating common symbolic resources. Language was made available for witty comment. Full of internal cross-referencing, the typical speech forms grew out of community solidarity and reinforced it. Relationships were more buffered; status within the positional family was more secure, so the members could afford more laughter and teasing. Breaches of position rules invite satire (when someone sits in the wrong chair: 'Who does she think she is?'). Each family would have its customized repertoire of quips. Role functions could be indicated obliquely (for example, by reference to the time of day).

Bernstein obviously loved the 'restricted code' best; he professed to be sorry for anyone who had no access to it. The speech was restricted only in the sense that it left most of its meanings to be carried non-verbally. It could be more condensed, briefer, more vivid, because its background was fixed and assumptions shared. His theory suited his own bias against the middle classes. I doubt whether mocking middle-class behaviour could have given offence to middle-class colleagues. It is in accord with LSE radicalism for professors to vaunt a lower social origin than is theirs in reality. Some fine distinction could be introduced here, for he himself was definitely born into the middle classes, but he had entered a profession, which put him a notch above his origins, or so he made out. Perhaps this was why his writing was so convoluted and abstract, so unlike the much praised restricted code. He used to joke wryly about his nomination by a writer in *New Society* as the sociologist whose jargon was the most difficult to read. Indeed, his writing is dense with technical terms, very elaborated. It is paradoxical that Bernstein's critics in socio-linguistics suspected him of bias against the underprivileged, a truly bizarre perversion of his attitude.

The linguists came against a different stumbling block, Bernstein's favourite word, 'code'. They could be comfortable talking about language as a code, but not about 'speech codes'. His colleagues tried to find codes in speech, and because they failed many linguists dismissed his work. In my opinion to look for speech coding on its own was naïve. If they wanted to demonstrate that Bernstein had or had not discovered two distinct kinds of speech, they should have tried to compare degrees of predictability, and the coherence and richness of syntax, to see whether the middle-class 'elaborated code' surpassed the 'restricted code' in these respects. At the same time, serious research would have had to take trouble to identify and test adults as well as children in the two kinds of community that would serve as experimental objects. If this more sophisticated testing were to be undertaken now, the task would be easier than in those pre-computer times, and I hope that it will be tried.

He was also suspected of determinism, cultural or linguistic: another complete misunderstanding. His theory drew a circle of dynamic interaction between permitted speech acts, which regulate what can be thought and done, and permitted behaviour, which feeds back onto the speech and transforms it in turn. Such misinformed objections would have faded out in a bigger arena.

As an anthropologist I was frankly an outsider to socio-linguistics. I listened agog and read avidly. Anthropologists' interest was in distinctive modes of thought, starting from Levy-Bruhl's idea of a primitive, pre-logical mentality,[4] and Cassirer's[5] distinction between mytho-poetic and rational instrumental thinking. Neither linguists nor anthropologists are required to know ancient languages and literatures. Now I find that in that very same period similar distinctions were being tried between kinds of speech and kinds of society, particularly in Classics. If anyone did know Auerbach's discussion[6] of syntactic and paratactic modes of writing they did not say so. It would have enriched Bernstein's programme to know of classical parallels that were being worked out at that very time. Marcel Detienne, in *Les Maîtres de la Verité*,[7] was contrasting two styles of thought and speech: the first, mythical thought, closed, religious, authoritative, where speech such as oaths and promises could have magical effects, and where speech was analogic; the second, dialogue speech, secular, the speech of the warrior group, open, words for argument and action, the thought practical and enquiring. Detienne organized his study of two forms of speech by comparing institutional structures, in a method closely parallel to Bernstein's own attempt to relate speech forms to social institutions. Though several scholars were working at the same time on this topic, I do not think they knew of each other's work. The same applies to later studies. The recent work of Hall and Ames applies Cassirer's distinctions to ancient Chinese texts, under the contrast between what they called correlative and causal thinking,[8] and I suspect if they were able to be applied to speech, we would recognize something close to the restrictive and elaborated codes.

I write this memoir because I have been so deeply influenced myself. I can fairly claim that I have tried to apply his ideas about speech, thought and social structure to the study of religion.[9] Bernstein was firing the first shots in a revolution in the social sciences. If the revolution has still not arrived it was no one's fault directly. It was due to normal parochialism in academia. He certainly enjoyed recognition in his lifetime, especially abroad, but it would have helped us all if the power and originality of his thinking had made a bigger impact. He started with speech and society, but it was a pity that he did not move on to take in culture. I hope it is not treasonable to suggest that socio-linguistics was not large enough a frame. If his ideas had been challenged and debated by the philosophers, classicists and orientalists to whose work his own applied, he and his theories would have gained greatly from the benefits of a larger shared community. But he did not want to expand his concerns. These other disciplines were interested in general questions about culture and understanding, while he insisted that his interest was in 'the transmission of culture' narrowly understood, that is, education. First and foremost he saw himself as an educationalist.

Notes

1   This is an amended version of the obituary that appeared in *The Guardian*, 27 September 2000.
2   Michael Young and Peter Wilmott, *Family and Kinship in East London* (London: Tavistock, 1956).
3   Elizabeth Bott, *Family and Social Network* (London: Tavistock, 1957).
4   Lucien Levy-Bruhl, *Primitive Mentality* (New York: Macmillan, 1922).
5   E. Cassirer, *Sprache and Mythos*. Translated by Suzanne Langer, *Language and Myth* (New York: Harper, 1945).
6   E. Auerbach, *Mimesis: The representation of reality in western literature* (Berne, Switzerland: A. Francke Ltd, 1946; Princeton, 1968).
7   M. Detienne, *Les Maîtres de la Vérité dans la Grèce Archaique* (Paris: Maspero, 1967).
8   D. Hall and R. Ames, *Thinking Through Confucius* (New York: SUNY, 1987); *Anticipating China* (New York: SUNY, 1995).
9   M. Douglas, *Natural Symbols, Explorations in Cosmology* (Harmondsworth: Penguin, 1970); *Leviticus as Literature* (Oxford: Oxford University Press, 1999).

BASIL BERNSTEIN

Prophet, teacher, friend

Paul Dowling, Culture, Communication and Societies, Institute of Education, University of London

IN THE FIELD OF social thought and research Bernstein was a prophet. His activities organized the field into sets of friends and enemies, colleagues, critics and acolytes that may well have been more or less equinumerous though not necessarily disjoint; that is what prophets do. There will, quite rightly, be no shortage of tributes to Bernstein the prophet from leading figures in the field.

A few of us were able to work closely and individually with him as his students. Oddly enough, whilst we may well be divided in our responses to his work proportionately to the divisions of the field as a whole, we are, I am sure, united in our recognition of the astonishing good fortune that brought us under his supervision.

As was the case with a number of his doctoral students, I was summoned by Professor Bernstein to discuss the possibility of research registration on the basis of something that he had identified in my master's dissertation (although reviewing the work now, I have to confess to being somewhat unclear as to what this 'something' might have been). Embarking on work on my thesis I found myself to be cast into a situation in which every aspect of my socio-logical knowledge – however well established its pedigree – every epistemo-logical presupposition, every tentative offer of empirical justification came under such vigorous and detailed interrogation that I felt as if I was experi-encing the intellectual equivalent of the osteopath's table: I was being taken apart, ossicle by ossicle. Furthermore, no region of the sociocultural terrain (and what else is there?) was immune from the Bernsteinian analytic gaze. Whatever took our attention in our weekly meetings would be minutely disassembled, reconfigured and ultimately recontextualized in a manner that inaugurated (although Basil would say revealed) the sententious in the mundane. What specialized sociology was not its object, but its privileging of relations and, in this, Basil was a true student of Marx.

Early on my writing would always begin with an extended contextualizing trip around what I perceived to be the relevant theoretical background. 'Where does it begin?' Basil would say as he flicked impatiently through ten pages that had taken several times as many hours to produce. 'At last', on page 11, 'some data, let's see what sense (if any) you've managed to make of it'. The ensuing display of theoretical coherence and analytic virtuosity was, initially, dazzling. But my career – managed and encouraged by the master – from the peripheral position of observer to the central one of active, even principal participant was (with deference to Jean Lave and Etienne Wenger) the quintessence of academic apprenticeship. Basil was not only a prophet, he was a teacher.

And, of course, there was more. Producing a doctoral thesis can be (almost inevitably is) a traumatic experience under any conditions. However stern his intellectual criticism, in the personal – I might say pastoral – context, Basil was thoughtful, considerate, concerned. When Basil asked 'How are you today?', I knew that he was genuinely interested in my answer: sympathetic and supportive in the troughs; celebratory at the peaks. The lunches that generally succeeded (although never truncated) the business part of our meetings continued and extended the wide-ranging social and cultural analyses that had characterized our earliest sessions before my work had developed its peculiar focus. I shall treasure these as amongst the most entertaining and warm social occasions that I have experienced in any context.

Even in its early stage of development – as instanced in my doctoral thesis – and most definitely now, my own work stands epistemologically and methodologically in a dialogic, which is of course to say a critical, relationship with Basil's and I reject the epithet 'Bernsteinian' as a descriptor of my position. Nevertheless, it is clear to me that his intellectual products and productivity have informed and shaped it in a manner the diversity and extent of which becomes increasingly apparent even at my present distance from the original thesis. Once, on re-reading one of his papers that I had previously referenced in 1986 I noticed a marked resonance with a position that I had been establishing some five years later. Intellectual arrogance directed my knee-jerk response and I remember thinking at first and with smug satisfaction that I had influenced him – until I looked at the date of publication.

First and foremost, however, what I hope Basil has given me (and what I know he has given to many others) is precisely the facility to develop coherence and systematicity in my own theoretical and methodological constructions.

That my own route contrasts with his has, delightfully, enabled me to continue my dialogic apprenticeship to him well beyond the supervision of my thesis and even beyond his death. I shall end this tribute by quoting from my acknowledgement to him in the thesis itself:

> The supervisor of this research was Professor Basil Bernstein. Basil brought to the supervision the stunning power of his own thought and work and an often devastating, but always constructive criticism of mine. This was combined with a level of commitment, in terms of time and care, that I cannot imagine being surpassed. The impact of this supervision upon the intellectual productivity, conceptual clarity and, indeed, the readability of this thesis is immeasurable, but immense.

Goodbye, Basil, and thank you.

SOCIOLOGICAL IMAGINATION

A tribute to Basil Bernstein

Tony Edwards, Emeritus Professor of Education,
University of Newcastle

I FIRST BECAME a student of the sociology of education when Basil Bernstein was beginning to teach it. At that time, the subject as defined in Britain was about social class and educational opportunity. It was high in social statistics and human interest, and hugely appealing to those who looked to sociological research to shape government policy towards greater equality of opportunity. But it lacked many connections to mainstream sociological theory. Bernstein transformed its scope and its ambitions. Within a few years his achievements dominated the subject in this country, represented abroad its most exciting direction, and stimulated many like myself to undertake their first substantial research within some part of his developing theoretical framework.

The stimulus was sometimes provocation as well as admiration. The originality and range of his thinking, shaped by extraordinarily wide reading in and beyond sociology, not only left his work open to the impoverished interpretations and misinterpretations about which he vigorously complained, but also tempted critics to seize on what they believed they could understand or which related most directly to their narrower research interests. In a long rebuke for my own misapplication of his work to the analysis of classroom practice, he charged me with 'rummaging among the attributes' for items convenient for my case.[1] I argued in response that it was unduly restrictive to insist that complex theoretical formulations should be used in their entirety or not used at all.

In practice however, his accounts of the social structuring of communication had led me from a doctoral study of social class differences in the speech of young children from contrasting areas of south Manchester, a study intended to 'test' the concept of codes, into a general review of research in the rapidly growing fields of socio-linguistics and the sociology of language. The book had a somewhat Bernstein-like title, *Language in Culture and Class* (1976), and his work dominated much of it. This experience will be similar to that of many who read him, were taught by him, or carried out research shaped by his ideas. It is the experience of being carried in far more ambitious directions than they would have taken otherwise by the force of his sociological imagination. It was an imagination which rejected the separation of structural from cultural explanations some time before structuration became a key sociological concept, and of intensive investigation of particular contexts from the 'macro-scopic orderings of society'. His capacity for making new connections could be spectacularly displayed in conversation, when it would often take flight in ways which left his listeners amazed – and struggling to keep up.

In his main work, he continued to grapple with the big ideas of European sociological discourse: the division of labour, changes in the economic and moral order, the distribution of power and control, and the cultural codes which regulate the transmission and reproduction of knowledge. That the grappling was usually presented at a high level of abstraction added to the difficulties of commentators struggling to construct a final version of an always-evolving theoretical framework. Bernstein once wrote that he was much more interested in 'the heuristic value' of his ideas than in even attempting to be definitive. In the article cited earlier he defended himself against my criticism of being too absorbed in refining the theory with the claim that 'there is nothing wrong in being abstract' provided that the abstractions are or become 'saturated with the concrete'.[2] There is a great deal wrong, however, with a theoretical (or 'mindless') empiricism. In many fields of sociological study to which he contributed, Bernstein made that kind of research much harder to justify. His great 'heuristic' contribution has been to both raise the level of sociological thinking about the inter-relations of social class, family and school, and to launch many researchers in many countries on the task of building on and testing those ideas.

Notes

1 A.D. Edwards (1987) 'Language codes and classroom practice', *Oxford Review of Education* 13: 237–47; Basil Bernstein (1994) 'Edwards and his language codes', *Oxford Review of Education* 20(2): 173–82; A.D. Edwards (1994) 'A reply to Basil Bernstein', *Oxford Review of Education* 20: 183–4.
2 Bernstein (1994): 180.

BERNSTEIN AND CATHOLICISM

Relationships visible and invisible

*Gerald Grace, Director for Research and Development
in Catholic Education, Institute of Education*

I shall start where Durkheim left off in his discussion of the Trivium/
Quadrivium and carry his analysis a stage further. I shall propose that the
Trivium is not simply about understanding the word, the principles which
lie behind it, the mechanics of language and reasoning, but is concerned
to constitute a particular form of consciousness, a distant modality of
the self.... To constitute that self in the Word, yes, but the Word of God.
A particular God. The Christian God.
(Basil Bernstein, *Pedagogy, Symbolic Control and Identity*, 1996, p. 84)

THE MATURE WORK of Bernstein returned to its Durkheimian origins in
making visible connections between the surface structures of contemporary
sociological phenomena and the deep structures of religious cultures,
doctrines and practices. In the realizations of knowledge and pedagogy,
language and social relations, institutional cultures and power relations, there
could still be found the imprint of religious thinking and the mediations of
religious practice. As Bernstein contemplated the course of cultural transformation over a long historical period he saw, with concern, the gradual domination of the marketized form of secularization:

Over the next five hundred years (from the medieval period) there was a
progressive replacement of the religious foundation of official knowledge by
a humanizing secular principle. I want to argue that we have for the first
time, a dehumanizing principle for the organization and orientation of

official knowledge.... Market relevance is becoming the key orientating criterion for the selection of discourses, their relation to each other, their forms and their research.

(Pedagogy, Symbolic Control and Identity, pp. 86–7)

With these observations Bernstein set in place an intellectually stimulating socio-historical and theoretical framework for studying the educational transformations of the sequence: transcendent religious principle → humane secular principle → market secular principle. His mature work provides a major theoretical resource for the analysis of contemporary Catholic culture and of the challenges faced by contemporary Catholic institutions, especially the schools.

During the course of a doctoral supervision, Basil Bernstein mentioned to me that if he ever took religion *really* seriously, i.e. as a believer and not simply as a sociologist of religious phenomena, he would become a Catholic. Uncharacteristically however, he did not elaborate this initial theoretical position but proceeded instead to the inquisition of a draft chapter of my thesis. I felt, at the time that the rapport he expressed with certain aspects of Catholic culture was interesting (and given his Durkheimian stance, not surprising) and as the supervision progressed I could see that he had a good understanding of a Catholic notion of an inquisition!

Bernstein's work, like that of his great mentor, Emile Durkheim in *The Elementary Forms of Religious Life* and in *The Evolution of Educational Thought*, has intellectually creative resonances with Catholic cultural forms, both historically and with their contemporary transformations. Catholic education, for instance, has been a paradigm case of the existence of strong classifications (sacred/secular; Catholic/non-Catholic) and of strong framing (traditional pedagogy; catechism instruction). Any researcher attempting to understand the transition of Catholic schooling to weaker forms of classification and framing will have to draw upon the luminous insights of Bernstein's work.

This applies also to the theoretically powerful concepts of visible and invisible pedagogy. Catholicism per se is a conjunction of the visible and the invisible and Catholic schools are necessarily engaged in activities which have visible outcomes and in activities which have relatively invisible outcomes. However, as Bernstein has pointed out, the visible pedagogy used by Catholic schools has always had 'the cover of the sacred'. This situation is now challenged by the emergence of market commodification of knowledge and the domination of a secular pedagogy.

In Bernstein's major text of 1996, *Pedagogy, Symbolic Control and Identity*, there are brilliant insights which illuminate the contemporary context for Catholic schools, the struggles they have to face and the contradictions in which they are located. In 'Pedagogizing knowledge' and in 'Thoughts on the Trivium and Quadrivium: the divorce of knowledge from the knower', Bernstein carried forward a classic analysis begun by Durkheim. This analysis demonstrates a conjunction of sociological, historical and theological under-standings which realize critical scholarship at its best. When Bernstein writes 'we are experiencing a truly secular concept of knowledge' (p. 4), he presents in condensed form the dilemma facing all faith-based schools in contempo-rary society. However, at the same time he bequeaths to all researchers the theoretical frameworks, theoretical concepts and above all the sociological imagination to engage with these dilemmas.

These thoughts have returned to me recently as I have struggled to give shape and form to my book-in-progress, *Catholic Schools: Mission, markets and morality*. The sociological study of Catholic education is remarkably undeveloped given that it is a worldwide schooling enterprise involving 120,000 schools which serve almost 50 million students in a range of socio-cultural and political settings. In particular, little attention has been given to applying aspects of social theory to a deeper understanding of the field of Catholic education. In chapter 2 of the book I have attempted to produce a more theorized account of Catholic education and schooling using perspec-tives from Bourdieu and from Bernstein.

From my first encounter with him in 1973 and subsequently throughout my academic career, Basil Bernstein has been for me the sociological imagi-nation made manifest. He had a quality of intellectual and personal vivacity which was stimulating to encounter. He has been a constant productive influence upon my own thinking, research and writing. If he had had that conversion experience he would have been an incredible animator of Catholic intellectual life and very quickly would have been in trouble with Rome (which he would have enjoyed). As it is, his unique theoretical imagination will animate and inspire Catholic education writers and researchers worldwide. The relationship between Bernstein and Catholicism will be recontextualized in the way he would have approved of, that is, in imagina-tive theorizing and in deep structural analysis of Catholic education in its various settings.

PROFESSOR BASIL BERNSTEIN AND THE INTERNATIONAL CENTRE FOR INTERCULTURAL STUDIES

Jagdish Gundara and Robert Ferguson,
International Centre for Multicultural Studies,
Institute of Education, University of London

THE INSTITUTE OF EDUCATION University of London initiated discussions about issues of racism and education at about the same time that the Inner London Education Authority started to focus on these issues in the mid-1970s.

The moving spirit at the Institute of Education was Professor Basil Bernstein, who proposed to the Academic Board and the Senate that the Institute set up a working party to examine the role that the Institute should play in dealing with racism within the education system. The working party, which he chaired, consisting of Institute staff as well as teachers, community leaders and activists was set up in 1976. It consulted widely with institutions, organizations and individuals on the role that the Institute could play in dealing with racism. Some of the organizations consulted included the many London Education Authorities, the Community Relations Commission, the Institute of Race Relations and activists and teachers from across Britain. The working party proposed the setting up of a Centre for Multicultural Education, which would have an institutional focus and work horizontally across the departmental structure as well as vertically through academic disciplines within the main departments of the Institute.

The working party's report was discussed widely within the Institute and an agreement was reached on the principle of setting up such a Centre. The Senate then set up a steering committee, which was also chaired by Professor

Basil Bernstein. It undertook detailed discussions about secondment of new staff from the Inner London Education Authority and from the Comparative, English and Sociology Departments of the Institute. The staff were to report to a co-ordinating committee chaired by a Pro-Director or a senior academic.

The Centre was duly set up in 1979 and has been a unique mechanism for dealing with issues of social diversity as they impact on education as well as dealing with racism at all levels of the Institute's work. However, Professor Bernstein also understood the ways in which institutions could carry out academic work in a few selected areas but ignore the deep-rooted issues of exclusivity within their institutional structures. He again demonstrated his understanding of the workings of the Institute by initiating the setting up of working parties, which through the early part of the 1980s examined the role that academic departments, administration and support staff needed to play in dealing with institutional racism.

These working parties dealt in detail with students' admissions, support for them within the Institute, administration structures and the ways in which all Institute staff needed to be knowledgeable about dealing with issues of racism at the institutional level. In academic terms the working parties' work was accepted by initial, higher degrees and research sub-boards. This institutional commitment was also publicly acknowledged in all the prospectuses of the Institute until the early 1990s.

This aspect of Professor Bernstein's commitment to the Institute and his grasp of the complexity of dealing with customs, procedures and practices within it that were inimical to providing equity in the field of higher education demonstrated not only his attachment to the institution but the breadth of his understanding and imagination of how inequalities become institutionally manifest. He always underplayed the grasp he had of issues of racism in education and the need to develop strategies to combat it. However he brought to bear his knowledge of institutional structures and social sciences to an area of work which has great international significance in the new millennium.

There was also passion in Professor Bernstein's approach to issues of racism and education. It was a passion which could hold you on the telephone for some time whilst he made it known that there was much work to be done. It did not matter whether he was dealing with the number of posters required to advertise an anti-racist activity, or with the exposition of a complex theoretical model. In the case of the former, Basil could invoke Durkheim and the concept of 'effervescence', explaining that such a quality was what was required amongst the rather staid responses to the outrage of racism that he sometimes perceived from his own institution. In regard to the latter, Professor Bernstein demonstrated a focused intellectual passion that commanded attention and respect. In committees he brought humour and political acuity to the business of the day and made the Academic Board a gathering that commanded the attention of the whole of the Institute. Basil was not perfect and did not pretend to be. One of his more memorable quips in committee was, 'I am nothing if not inconsistent'. There was, however, a consistency to his intellectual rigour and his passionate belief in opposing the racism that still plagues our society.

Professor Bernstein was totally at home at the University and in Bloomsbury. Over the years he made many friendships amongst his students and colleagues. He was a wonderful conversationalist and scintillating company and had a marvellous and ironical sense of humour. His delicacy, sartorial presence and gracious friendship, with a critical edge, will be much missed by his many friends and colleagues.

BASIL BERNSTEIN[1]

A.H. Halsey, Emeritus Fellow in Sociology,
Nuffield College, Oxford

BASIL BERNSTEIN was a marvellously impish man. He could reasonably be claimed to be the most thoughtful and inventive social scientist to emerge from the London School of Economics since the Second World War.

At that time, the LSE was still a home for outsiders, and Basil was one – born outside the metropolitan circle if, irrelevantly, near the Metropolitan line in the East End of London. If he went to grammar school, the experience completely failed to pigeonhole him, either as a Hogarthian scholarship boy or as the conventionally recognizable, successful literate or numerate, recruit to the professions.

Houghton Street and sociology gave him a fresh start, but his development was essentially one of autodidaction, and that again, through neither conquest of the foreign tongues nor quantitative skill, but, instead, by a remorseful and anguished inner conversation about his own social experience.

Among the unconventional consequences was his writing. It is unconventional in style, in form and in content. The prose is extremely difficult because, being an autodidact and not a traditionally learned man, and being an innovator rather than one who seeks to maintain an established conversation, Basil developed his own, if I may borrow one of his own inventions, 'elaborated code'.

I should add immediately, however, that he was enough of a positivist to seek to make big theories publicly available as empirically testable and refutable propositions.

The form of publication which he adopted was no less deviant from established English academic custom, which decrees that published work should be completed and written in a language shared by readers of the *Times Literary Supplement*.

These rules were part of the imprint of a public, or grammar-school, education. Basil did not so much flout as ignore them. He never hesitated to write down an incomplete theoretical argument, nor to publish a later version which was clearer or more developed. The underlying assumption always was that the journey mattered more than the destination.

Put in its most abstract form, Basil Bernstein's achievement was to make a serious attempt at surmounting the unending post-Hegelian debate on the relation between man's social consciousness and his material existence. It is true and important that, because of his work, the modern definition of the sociology of education is firmly centred on the analysis of pedagogical processes.

Note
1 This Appreciation was first printed in *The Guardian* on 29 September 2000.

BASIL BERNSTEIN,
AN EXCEPTIONAL

Ruqaiya Hasan, Emeritus Professor (Linguistics),
Macquarie University, NSW, Australia

I have made a deliberate choice to focus sharply upon the underlying rules shaping the social construction of pedagogic discourse and its various practices. I am doing this because I believe that sociological theory is very long on metatheory and very short on providing specific principles of description. I shall be concentrating ... on being able to provide ... models, which can generate specific descriptions. It is my belief that without ... [this, *RH*] there is no way in which we can understand the way in which these knowledge systems become part of consciousness.

(Bernstein 1996: 17)

IN OUR SAD BEREAVEMENT, we who have used Bernstein's theory – as well as those who will use it in the future – can take some comfort from the fact that Bernstein succeeded remarkably well in his aim of providing such models. The journey of enquiry which began in 1958 with 'Some sociological determinants of perception' – a slender paper of less than 20 pages – achieved its ultimate quest in 1990 with *The Structuring of Pedagogic Discourse*, Volume 4 of *Class, Codes and Control*. His early concern with the educational failure of a specific section of our society evolved by the logic of his own arguments into a concern with the failure of the official educational systems, and prepared the ground for providing rich models for describing the ways in which these systems are used to aid and abet the 'invidious' distribution of forms of consciousness, tipping the balance of power in favour of the dominating. And the pages of *Pedagogy, Symbolic Control and Identity* (1996) went on to examine critically the nature of the significant – some would say deplorable – changes that have inexorably enveloped the ethos of universities all over the world. With uncanny precision these pages predicted the implications of such changes for all who are involved with these places of learning.

In the course of this remarkable intellectual journey Bernstein's *oeuvre* has offered insights into important realms of our social existence: it has reached out to all those phenomena which impinge on his central problematic. It is for this reason that in a recent article (Hasan 1999) I described Bernstein's sociology as an *exotropic* theory – a type of theory whose primary allegiance is not to the mores of some recognized discipline: rather, it is committed first and foremost to the investigation and explication of its central problematic. As an exotropic theory, Bernstein's sociology treated its object of study not as something that is impermeable but as something that lived within and formed an active part of a society's designs for living. True to his precept that the nature of a category is not given by the relations *within* as much as by the relations *between* (Bernstein 1990), in the exploration of his central problematic Bernstein turned his attention to all those phenomena which appeared to form the context of the existence of his object of study and which acted as the means of its continued survival. Not surprisingly, the theory penetrates into the realms of semiotics, psychology, politics, education, to mention the most outstanding interconnections. An unbiased reading of Bernstein by scholars in any of these 'disciplines' will continue to pay high dividends. This is one outstanding measure of the exceptional nature of his achievement.

But simply making connections with another discipline by in some way referring to it is neither revealing nor a resource for future research. It seems to me that in each of these four major disciplines, Bernstein has made an exceptional contribution which illuminates the nature of that discipline's relation to the object of his study and offers an opening for further research. Take the relations of the social and the semiotic: Bernstein is not one of those sociologists who make a token bow in the direction of the semiotic, specifically the linguistic; nor does he appoint himself, unlike Bourdieu, as a referee in an imaginary wrestling match between the disciplines of sociology and linguistics. Treating semiotic practice as a subset of social practices he goes on to deconstruct its nature in a masterly manner in the very first chapter of the *Structuring of Pedagogic Discourse* (1990: 13–62). He reveals the dialectic of the social and the semiotic, whereby social practice without semiotic input is an impossibility and semiotic practice without its social context is a fiction of the formal linguist's imagination. Linguists who ignore this specific part of Bernstein's discourse do injustice to themselves and to their object of study. Bernstein's regard for Halliday's Systemic Functional Linguistics was simply because, of all the existing models, it was in this model that he noted efforts to integrate the social as an essential component of the theory of the semiotic.

For his seminal concepts Vygotsky is today deservedly the focus of attention in the discourses of social psychologists, cultural activity theorists and educationists. The enormously influential concept of *semiotic mediation* is particularly relevant to Vygotsky's ideas about the formation of consciousness (Vygotsky 1978). Bernstein arrived at similar insights long before Vygotsky became fashionable. Consider the following two extracts from the two:

> Every function in the child's cultural development appears twice: first on the social level, and later on the individual level; first *between* people (*interpsychologically*), and then *inside* the child *(intrapsychologically)*.... All the higher functions originate as actual relations between human individuals.
>
> (Vygotsky 1978: 57, original emphases)

> the particular forms of social relation act selectively upon what is said, when it is said, and how it is said ... [they] can generate very different speech systems or codes ... [which] create for their speakers different orders of relevance and relation.... As the child ... learns specific speech codes which regulate his verbal acts, he learns the requirement of his social structure. The experience of the child is transformed by the learning generated by his own, apparently, voluntary acts of speech.... From this point of view, every time the child speaks or listens, the social structure is reinforced in him and his social identity shaped. The social structure becomes the child's psychological reality through the shapings of his acts of speech.
>
> (Bernstein 1971: 144)

Bernstein's deep interest in the relations of the social and the semiotic complements Vygotsky's notion of semiotic mediation, permitting us to see its role in pluralistic societies both in the local and the official pedagogic contexts of discourse. In much of Vygotsky's writing, semiotic mediation appears as an essential means for the internalization of concepts and knowledge structures specific to the official pedagogic contexts. Bernstein's account provides an insight into how certain acts of semiotic mediation might be received differently by persons possessing different orders of relevance. I have argued elsewhere that no research involving the concept of semiotic mediation can afford to ignore what Bernstein had to say in this regard (Hasan 1993).

There has been much discussion on whether or not Bernstein was a Marxist. As he was to put it in his last book, such terms are a device for putting scholars and their theories into pre-categorized boxes, which is simply a varient of botanic labelling. The question is not whether Bernstein was a

Marxist; the significant point is what Bernstein made of Marx's ideas: how he developed them. In *The German Ideology*, Marx and Engels, asserting the primacy of 'material life-process', conclude that:

> Morality, religion, metaphysics, all the rest of ideology and their corresponding forms of consciousness, thus no longer retain the semblance of independence. They have no history, no development; but men, developing their material production and their material intercourse, alter, along with their real existence, their thinking and the products of their thinking. Life is not determined by consciousness, but consciousness by life.
>
> (Marx and Engels 1970: 47)

They claim 'empirical verifiability' for their hypothesis, but I believe I am not wrong in claiming that it was Bernstein who picked up the challenge implicit in this view. He transformed the simple linear 'dependence' into a powerful dialectic, and went on to show the trajectory of the relations of the material to the mental, of social interaction to consciousness. Having begun with the local and the concrete in the 1950s – why a certain group of children displayed a certain form of behaviour – Bernstein concluded his working life with an abstract and universal theory, capable of explaining not just that form of behaviour but its potential variants. This is indeed an exceptional achievement, for which the inheritors of his legacy will salute him with respect.

Basil Bernstein inscribed his last book to me playfully as follows: 'From one exceptional to another, with much gratitude for the years of our friendship. Basil.' In paying him my tribute I have rather inadequately tried to show that he truly was an exceptional – a generous friend, a great scholar, and an inspiring mentor.

References

Bernstein, Basil (1958) 'Some sociological determinants of perception', *British Journal of Sociology* IX: 159–74 (reprinted 1971 in *Codes, Class and Control: Vol. 1*. London: Routledge and Kegan Paul).

Bernstein, Basil (1971) *Class, Codes and Control: Vol. 1: Theoretical Studies Towards a Sociology of Language*. London: Routledge and Kegan Paul.

Bernstein, Basil (1990) *Class, Codes and Control: Vol. 4: The Structuring of Pedagogic Discourse*. London: Routledge: 13–62.

Bernstein, Basil (1996) *Pedagogy, Symbolic Control and Identity: Theory, research, critique*. London: Taylor and Francis.

Hasan, Ruqaiya (1993) 'Speech genre, semiotic mediation and the development of higher mental functions', *Language Sciences* 14 (4): 489–528.

Hasan, Ruqaiya (1999) 'Society, language and the mind: the meta-dialogism of Basil Bernstein's theory', in Frances Christie (ed.) *Pedagogy and the Shaping of Consciousness: Linguistic and social processes*. London: Cassell: 10–30.

Marx, Karl and Engels, F. (1970) *The German Ideology*. (Edited and Introduced by C.J. Arthur.) London: Lawrence and Wishart.
Vygotsky, L.S. (1978) *Mind in Society: The development of higher psychological processes*, edited by M. Cole, V. John-Steiner, S. Scribner and E. Souberman. Cambridge, MA: Harvard University Press.

FOR BASIL

Janet Holland, Professor of Social Research,
South Bank University, London

THIS YEAR IT HAS BEEN brought home to me all too forcefully how death stalks life. Two friends and mentors have died of a monstrous disease whilst in full flow of their mental and personal capacities. It is hard to accept that they are dead, that all that brilliance is gone. Thankfully at least for each their vision can live on in their work; they have that memorial, and our endless remembering. The last time I sat down to write something about Basil was on the day I learned of Caroline Benn's death.

Then as now I found it hard to write about Basil. There is his work, with its boundless fecundity, growing in our minds and in our own research and practice, spinning off into routes we could not have imagined alone. I remember the struggle I had with his language when I first joined the Sociological Research Unit in 1976, reading the piles of papers he had produced. I tried to keep up with the twists and turns as subtle changes, sometimes all but invisible to the naked eye, pushed a new version of an argument on into clearer territory. I rejoiced in each edition of *Class, Codes and Control*, where an introduction thoughtfully helped to bring us up to speed.

There is his supervision. His generosity to his students and fantastic capacity to know more about your data than you knew yourself is quite rightly legendary. I recalled that we struggled, as I endeavoured to bring gender and feminist theory into the frame, fearing that the feeble shoots of my thoughts would wither in the heat of his ferocious intellect. But, should I take my thesis from the shelf these days, I cannot help but see the fruits of his generosity in letting those shoots bloom (if that is not pushing the metaphor too far!) and the way the work is clearly my own, as well as clearly the result of learning from and using his insights and skill.

There is his friendship, rocky though that path has sometimes been. But it was also a hell of a lot of fun: a gossip, a witty deconstruction of a mutual

132

friend or acquaintance, a drink, a wonderful meal, a searing critique of your latest piece which omitted to recognize the importance of his influence.

And there is his influence, with which I live every day. Every piece of research I do is based at core on what I learned at Basil's knee and I will always be grateful for all that he has meant in my life.

BASIL BERNSTEIN

*Dell Hymes, Commonwealth Professor of Anthropology
and Commonwealth Professor of English, Emeritus,
University of Virginia, Charlottesville, USA*

FORTY YEARS AGO sociolinguistics could hardly be said to exist. It was almost merely the filling of a verbal paradigm:

Ethnology	:	ethnolinguistics
Psychology	:	psycholinguistics
Sociology	:	?

Here and there in Europe and America there were individuals who saw the desirability, once might say the necessity, of an approach to language from the standpoint of social realities, alert to the details of language, but as organized in terms of social situations and relations. In Great Britain the linguistic tradition of Firth encouraged such alertness, and Michael Halliday developed a descriptive approach in just such terms. And there was Basil Bernstein, addressing realities of language in social life, attentive to class and to what occurs in schools.

It was natural that people like myself and John Gumperz, eager to see such approaches grow, would seek out Basil, would see in Basil a rare beacon of light within a horizon where beacons were few and far between. Basil and his work loomed large then, and I venture to say will continue to loom large, wherever the organization of language in terms of relations shaped by class is of concern. Since class shows no sign of fading away, that is likely to be a very long time.

PROFESSOR BERNSTEIN'S LEGACY TO JAPAN

Yoshiyuki Kudomi,
Professor of the Sociology of Education,
Hitotsubashi University, Kunitachi City, Tokyo

PROFESSOR BERNSTEIN came to Japan in 1993 upon the invitation of the Faculty of Social Sciences at Hitotsubashi University, which I had delivered to him two years earlier. It was his second visit to Japan. During his stay in Tokyo – about ten days – he gave three public lectures in our University on 'Cultural reproduction', 'Pedagogic code' and 'Pedagogic device'. Before arriving in Japan, he had sent us two papers, one each for his second and third lectures. We translated them into Japanese and prepared the Japanese translations as handing-out material for the audience of his lectures.

When I was telling him about the translated material, he suddenly said that it was sufficient for the audience to have material and it would be stupid for him to lecture according to it. He also said that he would like to lecture using new drafts of a different plan. I advised him that it might be better to lecture from the original papers because, though Japanese scholars and students were interested in his theory, it was not easy for them to understand and they are usually not very good in speaking and listening to English. So, I thought, it would be very useful for them to have the translated material. But even so he insisted on lecturing the same themes using new drafts.

His first lecture was given on 'Cultural reproduction' according to his handwritten paper, which he had brought from England. As for the other two lectures, he had to spend time writing the new drafts in his hotel room. During that time he often questioned me on the nature of research in the sociology of education in Japan and the main interest of Japanese academics. He changed the content of his drafts several times before my very eyes. It took almost two and half days for him to prepare the second lecture on 'Pedagogic code' and one and half days for the third lecture on 'Pedagogic device'. In the afternoon of the day before the third lecture, after finishing writing the new draft, he said to me, 'I came to Japan at this time in order to write new papers' with a wry smile. In fact until that time he had not even been to the famous and beautiful park which is just near the hotel and which could be seen from his window.

These three lectures were very successful. They were exciting and the audiences gradually increased from the first to the third as they gained in popularity. It was a great opportunity for Japanese scholars of the sociology of education to receive his theory of pedagogy in the 1980s and 1990s. Those who had been responsible for inviting him were very surprised at and full of admiration for his sincerity and eagerness in preparing his lectures – even in a foreign country of the Far East. I also thanked him for his kindness and understanding in allowing us to hand out the translated material to the audience.

After his return to England a group, myself included, was set up in order to study his theory on pedagogy. When I wrote to him in England to tell him of this, he answered by recommending that we make the Japanese translation into a new book, editing his lecture notes and other papers. He gave our translation group not only the lecture notes but also several new papers, which were eventually published in England in 1996 as *Pedagogy, Symbolic Control and Identity*. However, we started to read and translate them in 1994. Hosei University Press in Tokyo decided to publish the Japanese translation.

The work of translating his book was very hard for the translation group, which was composed of five members. Not only to translate English into Japanese but to understand the theoretical logic in his book was a very, very difficult task for us. Sometimes it took one or two hours to understand and translate only one sentence. After a long struggle, at the end of spring 1999, we presented the publisher with the final drafts of translation. We received the first galley at the beginning of that autumn. But then from that point it took almost a year to perfect the galleys. The more we analysed the translation and compared it with his theories, the more dissatisfied we were with our attempts to relay his work accurately into Japanese. During these two years I wrote to him about such delay and apologized several times. He answered by thanking and encouraging us in our efforts to pursue a better translation.

At last, however, by the fourth version we felt in ourselves that by repeatedly checking we had not only been able to achieve our ultimate goal in translation but had experienced an extraordinary chance to see so closely into his theory and its great importance for educational research in Japan.

I was able to inform him on 10 September 2000 that his book would finally be published in Japan in the following month, and in answer to this he sent me an email message on 14 September. I was elated to read the following:

> Dear Prof Kudomi,
>
> Many, many congratulations on the translation of *Pedagogy, Symbolic Control and Identity* to be published in October 2000. It has been an amazing effort, pursued with utter diligence and extraordinary commitment. I do not think such a translation with such conviction could have been presented by any other group. It is my one great hope that your work will be recognized and appreciated for what it is: a distinguished contribution to sociology.
>
> With all good wishes,
> Basil Bernstein.

At that time my fellow translation group members and I were given tremendous encouragement from this message, not knowing or expecting that this would be our last communication with Professor Bernstein. For only ten days later we were to hear the sad news of his passing away. Our great regret is that he could not be with us together to celebrate the publication of his book only twenty days later.

In Japan at present I think the specifically Japanese style of schooling and teaching has reached a sort of standstill. Professor Bernstein's legacy to us in Japan is, most of all, his theory itself on pedagogy, which I strongly believe to be very useful and of enormous value to us in analysing theoretically and empirically the nature of the standstill in education which we find today. This legacy is his greatest gift to us in Japan.

BASIL

A personal tribute

John Mace, Senior Lecturer, Institute of Education,
University of London

I MET BASIL in the coffee room, sadly long since closed, of Gordon Square in January 1972. I had no idea who he was, but was delighted when he invited me to join in the 'gossip' of the group with whom he was talking. This first meeting indicated two things about Basil: his openness and willingness to include 'outsiders', for that I certainly was, and his interest in non-academic matters – qualities that endured until his death. By the afternoon Basil and his research colleagues had decided that I should be invited to join them in a drink at the Marlborough, the favourite watering hole at that time. It was in the discussions taking place there that I learned two further things: that Basil had a brilliant and inventive mind, one reason why so many people were to be found clustered around his table, and was reminded that being in an inn often provided a stimulus to intellectual discourse that would not necessarily be reproduced in a seminar room. It would be disingenuous of me not to admit that much of the 'sociology' was way beyond me. It is a tribute to Basil that so many of those who were to be found in the Marlborough at that time remained friends with him for the rest of his life.

Others have spoken of his willingness to give intellectual support, however time-consuming; for me it was perhaps as important that he was so willing to provide friendship and support in at least equal measure to colleagues and friends. Like so many others, he was always ready to provide critical comment on anything that I was bold enough to invite him to read. This was particularly the case when I was writing my thesis under his supervision. My effusive acknowledgement to him in the thesis did not do justice to the role that he played in that particular endeavour. I know other students experienced similar support, guidance and motivation. We all know that Basil was a genius, but he was also a scholar (although he always denied it) and he encouraged scholarship at every opportunity, perhaps realizing, though never saying, that this was the best the rest of us could aspire to.

I know that Basil always claimed that early in his career he worked as a PE and English language teacher, but I have cause to doubt this because it would suggest he had a sense of balance and a mastery of the meaning of English words. My evidence: many were the times I would take him back to Dulwich, his home, on my motorcycle. This was always a slightly worrying time, particularly when wet, as Basil tended to lean in the wrong direction when going round bends. Occasionally, after Marion had generously provided us with a strong drink, I would express my concerns about the dangers of him doing this; to which he would reply 'but I'm ambidextrous'! This was a man of humour, as well as wit, scholarship and genius. He was a great friend and a great man and I shall miss him always.

BASIL BERNSTEIN AND
SOCIAL THEORY

Rob Moore, Reader in Sociology of Education,
Homerton College, Cambridge

I FIRST MET Basil Bernstein in 1967 when I was an undergraduate at what was then Borough Polytechnic. Like so many others, I was hooked from the beginning by his virtuoso display of brilliance. That brilliance remained with him to the end and over that long period of time he remained a generous and inspiring teacher who was always happy to welcome me back however long the gap between our meetings. I remember him with the greatest respect, affection and gratitude.

The appreciations of Bernstein, both in the volumes published in his honour before his death and the tributes that have followed it, have most often taken the form of examples of the amazing variety of research that his theory has generated worldwide. This would be pleasing to him because his own concern was that the theory should *work* in the sense of being capable of being *put to work* and creating 'news'. To a significant degree, the fact that Bernstein's theory could generate such a variety of research is to do with the *kind* of theory that it is. But what kind of theory is it? How can we characterize Bernstein's theory and how can we locate it within the sociological tradition and in terms of current debates? This is not straightforward. Although he was clear about his debt to Durkheim, and on various occasions indicated the sources that comprised his 'intellectual matrix', nowhere did he provide a systematic summary of his theory (though see Bernstein and Solomon 1999). Bernstein was a social theorist of the first rank, but his theory remains enigmatic. A major task on his passing is that of exegesis – not as a scholastic exercise, but in order to display and learn from the great originality of his synthesis.

In his aspiration to produce a major theoretical system, Bernstein was unusual in British sociology. In the second half of the twentieth century, only

Giddens is generally acknowledged as having attempted to create a *theory*. By contrast, Ernest Gellner, a social theorist of immense intellectual power and originality, appears to be virtually ignored except in specialist areas such as nationalism, where he made a seminal contribution, but one that by no means exhausts the scope and potential of his ideas for other areas, including the sociology of education. Bernstein is recognized as a theoretician, but we lack a clear sense of the character of the theory. The British have a problem with theory: it is something that foreigners do, hence we look abroad for it.

It is ironic that the contemporary enthusiasm in the anglophone academic world for French theory seems largely unconscious of the degree to which a thinker such as Foucault is so deeply entrenched in the Durkheimian legacy (in effect it was Durkheim's critique of humanism that announced 'the death of the subject', but in a way that provides a crucial alternative to the Nietzschean nihilism that blights post-structuralism) and so blind to the contribution of the most authentically Durkheimian of anglophone theorists. Durkheim is, of course, central to understanding Bernstein's theory. But simply to name Bernstein as a 'Durkheimian' is not to provide an answer to the question of what kind of theory Bernstein gave us, because understanding Durkheim is itself highly problematic. As Bernstein points out on a number of occasions, Durkheim was radically recontextualized in Anglo-Saxon social theory by a received Parsonian reading that was then incorporated into the field-positioning strategies of the positivist debate and the critique of functionalism of the late 1960s and early 1970s (of which the New Sociology of Education came to be a part).

Bernstein writes of Durkheim's 'magnificent insight' (1973) and the key to understanding Bernstein's theory is to appreciate his own magnificent insight into Durkheim. He had a remarkable understanding of Durkheim that informed his thinking from the beginning, from his time at LSE. It was an understanding derived from *The Elementary Forms of Religious Life* (Durkheim 1995) and reflected in his abiding interest in religion and in the work of British structural anthropologists such as Edmund Leach and Mary Douglas (who were both friends; the latter, in her book *Natural Symbols* (1970), provided one of the most original and sophisticated applications of classification and framing in terms of the relationship between cosmology and social structure). Conventionally, Durkheim as the conservative social order theorist is contrasted with Marx, the theorist of revolutionary change. Bernstein knew that this view is as limited as that which brands Durkheim a 'positivist'. Durkheim was not a conservative either in politics or theory and as a Kantian rationalist he mounted a sustained sociological critique of positivist empiricism; this was at the heart of his work. What is most striking about Marx and Durkheim is not their differences but the similarities between their particular brands of historical materialism – between Marx, say, of the *Economic and Philosophic Manuscripts* and what Bourdieu calls 'the Durkheimian philosophy of man' (1990).

Understanding Bernstein's theory involves a wider view of the field of social theory: of its lineages and the relationships between its key figures. He includes Marx and Mead within his 'intellectual matrix', but does not provide a detailed exposition of precisely how he understands and uses these classical theories and synthesizes elements from approaches that might more conventionally be treated as incompatible. As far as Durkheim is concerned, there is now a developing body of interpretation that radically challenges the received view, and does so in a way that is illuminating as far as Bernstein is concerned (see for instance Collins 2000, ch. 1, especially p. 22). The synthesis represented by Bernstein's 'matrix' is highly original, but inevitably, not entirely unique. The structure of the matrix becomes clearer when observed from a perspective where others are making similar connections to those that shaped Bernstein's approach. The task of theoretical exegesis is an important one, first because the originality of his synthesis was one of his major contributions, and, secondly, because of the manner in which he developed and extended theory in his own right.

Although Bernstein never cared to label his theory, he nevertheless continually *displayed* its form in his work. In this respect there is, I think, a parallel between his writing and his teaching style. Always, as my teacher, Basil rarely stated directly, he laid things in front of me and asked, 'Do you *see*?' This was the most demanding pedagogic discipline, but also the most rewarding when I did 'see' and he would laugh in delight and applaud. He was the master of intellectual creativity and creativity was his greatest delight. He sent me an early draft of what was to become 'Vertical and horizontal discourse: an essay' (Bernstein 1999). I read this with great interest and made notes. We met and went for lunch in the bar of the Russell Hotel. I expounded upon his distinction between internal and external languages of description. At a certain point he lent forward and patted my hand, 'Actually,' he said, 'it's the other way around'. I realized to my horror that I'd got it completely back to front! 'But do go on', he said, 'This is so interesting.' He was both the most rigorous and least dogmatic of thinkers. The key to the exegesis of Bernstein's theory is to *see* what he is doing – to read the brilliant display he presented to us.

References

Bernstein, B. (1973) *Class, Codes and Control: Vol. 1*. London: Routledge and Kegan Paul.
Bernstein, B. (1999) 'Vertical and horizontal discourse: an essay', *British Journal of Sociology of Education* 20 (2): 157–74.
Bernstein, B. and Solomon, J. (1999) 'Pedagogy, identity and the construction of a theory of

symbolic control: Basil Bernstein questioned by Joseph Solomon', *British Journal of Sociology of Education* 20 (2): 265–80.

Bourdieu, P. (1990) *Homo Academicus*. Cambridge: Polity.

Collins, R. (2000) *The Sociology of Philosophies: A global theory of intellectual change*. Cambridge, MA: Harvard University Press.

Douglas, M. (1970) *Natural Symbols: Explorations in cosmology*. London: Barrie and Rockliff.

Durkheim, E. (1995) *The Elementary Forms of Religious Life*. New York: Free Press.

THEORY AND DESCRIPTION

Bernstein and the dynamics of research

Gemma Moss, Research Officer, Policy Studies,
Institute of Education, University of London

NEWSPAPER OBITUARIES are peculiar texts, and Basil Bernstein's were no exception. Of course, who the newspaper asks to write them, the length of time the obituary has lain on the file, the physical space that the obituary can fill on any given day, all play their part in shaping the genre. As someone who had the privilege of working with Bernstein, I looked for a picture of the person I knew, and some recognition of the excitement of the scope of his ideas. More often than not one found a reductive, even parsimonious account of his work, hinging round restricted and elaborated codes, a static version of Bernstein already entombed in a long dead history. Fred Inglis's piece in *The Independent* was a notable exception.

Of course, newspaper obituaries are designed for a non-specialist audience. They don't set out to sample from the current state of debate within academe. That is not their function. Nevertheless, reading the obituaries somehow underlined for me the way in which Bernstein's work is so often misread. Not so much in terms of the misappropriation of individual parts of his theory, though the misuse of 'restricted' and 'elaborated' code by linguists in the 1970s remains a shameful case in point, but rather its misrepresentation as an overly complex endeavour, a closed, theoretical edifice of baroque proportions, which allows of no dialogue: either one accepts it all and becomes a slave to its categories, or one can find no use for the thing. The label 'structuralist', which Basil fiercely objected to, was perhaps a polite way of trying to box him in in these terms, simultaneously recognizing his scope, and yet explaining why the theory must be consigned to a historical byway, passed over by more modern, post-structuralist concerns.

My experience of working with Basil tells a different story. In particular what I want to write into the record is the powerful, generative quality of his thinking. The principles of Basil's work may indeed have remained largely unchanged since the earliest days – he was certainly fond of saying so – but their application to the shifting terrain of the times always allowed for a reworking, re-integration, and re-focusing of the territory, in exciting and dynamic ways. Indeed, the constant revision of his work in which he was engaged, is a testament to this creativity.

Where this aspect of his work comes across most clearly is in his speci-fication of the intellectual endeavour as the construction of a language of description. For Bernstein, this is a rigorous undertaking with precise rules of engagement. These he laid down in his paper 'Research and languages of description', published in *Pedagogy, Symbolic Control and Identity* (Bernstein 1996). Basil handed me the phrase 'evolving a language of description' as an aim for the research process early on in my career as a researcher. I took the phrase onboard long before I really understood what it might fully mean, because it captured something that I felt about the data I was then dealing with. I recognized that the way in which I described the data made a profound difference to what I took it to be, how I understood it and indeed how I theorized about it. Bernstein puts the point most succinctly like this:

> I would ... say that principles of description construct what is to count as empirical relations, and translate those relations into conceptual relations. A language of description constructs what is to count as an empirical referent, how such referents relate to each other to produce a specific text, and translates these referential relations into theoretical objects or potential theoretical objects.   (Bernstein 1996: 136)

Here at once is the move between description and theory: for Bernstein the act of description is always theoretical. To acknowledge this from the outset is to begin to control the process of evolving theory from description and vice versa in a more principled and motivated way than would otherwise be possible. It is the dialogic move between the two that Bernstein emphasizes. The researcher must be 'prepared to live with the muddle which is the unordered data, and enjoy the pleasure of its potential, in order to be able to generate the theoretical apparatus which is specific to it' (Bernstein, personal communication). Get in there too soon with the theory and it will overwhelm the data, limiting its potential to say something new. Delay pulling back from the data too long, and the researcher runs the risk of ending up submerged in the specifics, with no way of identifying the general principles which underpin the whole.

It is the general principles, the 'what makes the data tick', that Bernstein always prioritizes. His way of getting at this was to look at the relations between data. The way the researcher groups the data, and thereby categorizes it through description, makes those relations visible. The relations between categories then point to something else – the underlying rules or principles which generate the particular instance. In these respects, Bernstein likens the ethnographers' enterprise to learning a language:

> The researcher has first to learn the language of the group or society and know the rules of its contextual use ... to grasp how members construct their various texts or manage their contexts. The problem is to construct the tacit model. If the researcher fails to construct the model s/he is marooned in the specific contexts and their enactments, is in no position to appreciate the potential of ... that particular culture and thus its possible enactments. Without a model, the researcher can never know what could have been and was not.
> (Bernstein 1996: 137–8)

In these respects, for Bernstein a language of description must always have two faces: what he calls an external face pointing out to the empirical instances, or enactments; and an internal face, pointing to the inner logic which makes the performance possible. In the published paper he calls these respectively L2, the external language of description; and L1, the internal language of description. In discussion, he sometimes used the terms 'language of enactment' and 'language of explanation' to define these different orientations. There are shades here of a kind of Chomskyan distinction between surface and deep grammar; or a Saussurean distinction between parole and langue. The confines of a tightly bound structuralist paradigm raises its head. But by sharply delineating these two distinct functions of any language of description and making them explicit, what Bernstein is really doing is calling researchers to account. For L2 remains the interface between the researcher's language and the empirical realization of the object under scrutiny. It acts as a check and balance to L1, so that the latter cannot spin out of control, under the force of its own internal logic. The two languages must be constructed together, argues Bernstein, and in relation to each other, but they must never become conflated. L2 must retain its integrity, and its outward-facing role:

> L2, the external description, irrespective of the translation demands of L1 ... must as far as possible, be permeable to the potential enactments of those being described. Otherwise their voice will be silenced. From this point of view, L2, the external description, becomes an interpretive interface, or the

means of dialogue between the agency of enactments and the generating of the internal language of the model.   (Bernstein 1996: 138)

What is compelling about this account is its elegance and its efficiency, but also its generative possibilities. The concept of evolving a language of description provides an immediate handle on what the theoretical enterprise might be, and how it can be built in relation to the data. Indeed, my understanding of the principles of theory building, and the criteria by which theory can be tested; the capacity to build generative theory, and the methodological issues at stake in attempting this, directly stems from my reading of Bernstein's paper on languages of description in *Pedagogy, Symbolic Control and Identity* (Bernstein 1996).

Reference

Bernstein, B. (1996) 'Research and languages of description', in *Pedagogy, Symbolic Control and Identity: Theory, research, critique*. London: Taylor and Francis.

FOR BASIL

Joe Muller, Professor of Education,
University of Cape Town, South Africa

BASIL BERNSTEIN was first known to us here in South Africa, as he was to the rest of the world outside the UK, as the deficit hypothesis man who had received the worst of it in a notorious exchange with Labov, and who served primarily as a negative pole from which we, following a vanguard of self-styled fellow radicals, could extol the virtues of non-standard English and the exciting possibilities of resistance theory, thereby comprehensively missing his main point. That, through the long dark 1980s under apartheid, is what we taught our trainee teachers, and I suppose we may even have believed it. But, we had other fish to fry at the time, and we fished very selectively in global theoretical waters for ammunition to bolster discursively the burgeoning revolt in the schools and the streets, which hardly needed support from us. Classification and framing somehow didn't quite fit the bill.

By the turn of the decade, things had changed, and along with many others, we began to read Bernstein seriously again. The triumphalist mood in the country, our initial policy ardours included, had not taken long to cool, and copies of *Class, Codes and Control, Volume 4* began circulating (probably the most poorly distributed book in the history of the sociology of education and a publishing scandal). So when in October 1994 our annual Kenton conference (an annual forum for critical educational thought) was to celebrate its twentieth birthday, we paired it with an invitation to Basil to deliver both the keynote at the conference and a seminar series to a small group of senior students and scholars. The seminar series covered the main chapters of what was to become Volume 5, and it was a revelation, both in style and content. None of us had seen Basil in action before, and we were given a crash course into the exquisite rigours of what we didn't quite realize then was a new Bernsteinian direction – on knowledge structure and identity. Basil was in top form and the seminar was transfixed. There was no question that we had now grasped the point, and an entire generation of PhD students here has become creatively fired by the extraordinary paper on knowledge structure. Not only has it sparked research in the schools, but it has been influential in debates around national curriculum reform, and programme planning in higher education. (When told early in 2000 that his conceptual framework formed the basis for a government review into the national curriculum, Basil's response was typical: he courteously complimented the formulators, but declined responsibility, or interest. For one so influential on a conceptual framework for thinking about discourse and knowledge, Basil has displayed absolutely no interest in influencing educational policy.)

It has always struck me as extraordinary that the old Bernstein hands, with honourable exceptions, have refrained from following Basil into discussions on knowledge. In his last mimeographed paper circulated at the Lisbon Bernstein seminar in June 2000 Basil described the research programme projected by a 'sociology of pedagogy' as having become restricted and restrictive, and described his recent work aimed at grasping our emergent discursive culture under the rubric of a 'sociology for the transmission of knowledges'. It was this direction he spelt out to us in that first mesmerizing Bernsteinian seminar in 1994. It could be said then that at a happily synchronous point when we in South Africa had reached something of a theoretical cul de sac, and he himself had taken, for quite different reasons, the turn to knowledges, Basil rounded our Cape for the first time.

Or so we thought. Not according to Basil. First we heard that he'd been stationed here during the war, and had hitchhiked regularly to Alexandria, a township bordering Johannesburg, to give literacy classes to adults. Then we heard that he had once walked to the top of Table Mountain and left a poem there under a rock (you can imagine, delivered with a thin gleam of challenge, to find it if we dared). And then, somewhat more murkily, that he had come within a hair's breadth of becoming the manager of a sugar farm for a Natal sugar baron. Could any of this be true? Did it matter? We were entranced; the Swiss restaurateur's wife was entranced (serving us yet another bottle of champagne long after the restaurant had closed and her husband had gone home, this on the night of his 70th birthday: chipper as always the next morning at the seminar, of course). Conceptually, this small community here would take a while to recover.

Basil returned for a second seminar series in July 1997, with some misgivings, since he had, he said, nothing really new to show us. This was true in the sense that he had not taken another huge conceptual leap as he had the previous time, but what he showed us the second time round was the path he had taken in refining his concepts since their first presentation to us in 1994.

This was fascinating in another way, and allowed us another kind of glimpse into the workings of a brilliant and creative mind. And was there no disjuncture, no cultural jarring that took place in transporting Bernstein to the colonies, so to speak? Never once, not even for a moment. Always and in every way the dapper and cultivated Londoner, Basil's intellectual comportment was in the best possible way universal. Basil's work is a gift, calling forth the reciprocal injunction to share in the work.

I notice I have written above in a rather impersonal third person. That is because I find it difficult – no, I find it impossible to speak personally about Basil in public. I will honour him in the work, in the mutual joy of understanding. In this true community, where there are no prophets, Basil has a special place for ever.

FOUR THINGS I LEARNT
FROM BASIL BERNSTEIN

Sally Power, Professor of Education,
Institute of Education, University of London

BASIL BERNSTEIN has been the key source of intellectual inspiration throughout my academic career. In this short tribute I want to identify four aspects of his work that have been very important to me:

- a recognition of the significance of form as well as content
- the importance of counter-factuality in explanations
- the need to study education systems as phenomena in their own right
- the irrelevance of prevailing fashion for good sociological analysis.

The significance of form

I clearly remember reading Basil's paper 'On the classification and framing of educational knowledge' when I was an undergraduate (Bernstein 1977). Even though it had been published for over ten years and was widely recognized as a seminal text by the time I came across it, it opened up for me a way of looking at schooling that was entirely novel and completely compelling. Indeed, his invitation that we examine the curriculum 'in terms of the principle by which units of time and their contents are brought into a special relationship with each other' was the main impetus behind my undertaking a PhD.

Basil's use of dichotomous distinctions and analytical quadrants is not just elegant; it invites a focus on underlying properties that can be challenging and insightful. His seemingly endless diagrammatic 'models' open up so many possibilities for comparisons over time and space. Overhead transparencies of these went with me to Argentina in 1997 when I visited the University of Cordoba on a British Council Fellowship to give a series of lectures on Basil's 'analisis espistimologico'. I can think of few other models that could so effectively facilitate analysis of the relative properties of the Argentinian and English education systems and of the changing relations between state and church in the battle for symbolic control.

The importance of counter-factuality

Although most of Basil's writing concerns theoretical and conceptual development, he laid great store on the importance of empirical evidence. As he so cogently argued in his critique of the sociology of education (1977), many sociological interrogations are often concerned only with the approach rather than the value of the explanation. In his critique of the 'approach paradigms', he outlined how 'theories are less to be examined and explored at conceptual and empirical levels, but are to be assessed in terms of their underlying models of man and of society'. Indeed, he argued that '[t]he very form such questioning may take may obscure our understanding' (1977: 157). Theoretical adequacy does not rest on having the 'correct' ideological position but on its engagement with empirical research. As he put it: 'any theory is only as good as the principles of description to which it gives rise' (1992: 5–6). His claim of 25 years ago that we need 'less allegiance to an approach, and more of a dedication to a problem' (1977: 171) remains just as valid today.

Understanding rather than transforming education

Although Basil was concerned to point out the structures and processes that create and contribute to educational inequalities, his project was much broader – the study of education transmissions and systems as phenomena in their own right. He might perhaps disagree, but I think his analyses encourage us to understand the world, not necessarily to change it. They are primarily about elucidation rather than transformation.

While some might see this as essentially conservative, I think it yields far better insights than many 'crusading' sociological analyses – which are often based on simplistic oppositions that do not grasp the complexity of the processes.

The blindness of such oppositions when tied to value positions rather than inherent properties is brilliantly illustrated in Basil's exposition of invisible pedagogies (1977). His dissection of the tacit rules of control (made so accessible with his four lavatories analogy) is surely a salutary warning of the dangers of ideological and oppositional beliefs such as traditional=bad and progressive=good.

Not a follower of fashion

His adherence to evidence and explanation rather than to ideological approach was a contributory factor in the demonizing of his work on languages. The first time I came across Basil's work was as an undergraduate when we covered the Bernstein v. Labov debate. I remember that session very clearly: the general presumption that Labov was right and Bernstein was not only wrong but a collaborator in the myth of (white) middle-class superiority.

At that time, it was unfashionable to take the attributes of middle class-language seriously and to analyse them as something other than the background against which to celebrate working-class culture. When the evidence is re-examined and the orthodoxies questioned (Bernstein 1996), the appropriateness of such analysis seems self-evident. At times, it seems that Basil was one of the very few people to move outside the frame and identify how the biases in the field lead to distortion and omission. Twenty-five years ago, he was one of the few people to call for research into the social reproduction of the middle-class. Yet, it is only until recently that the middle class has featured within the sociology of education as anything other than the symbol of success against which the structural disadvantages of others are compared.

To conclude, Basil Bernstein stood out in the field as a powerful advocate for a sociology of education that has integrity – one that seeks to scrutinize rather than follow fashion and one that upholds the importance of empirical evidence without sacrificing theory.

References

Bernstein, B. (1992) 'Code theory and research, Vol. 5', unpublished paper to appear as (1993) *Code Theory and Research for the Sociology of Education* [in Spanish], Barcelona: El Roure.

Bernstein, B. (1977) *Class, Codes and Control: Vol. 3*, 2nd edn. London: Routledge and Kegan Paul.

Bernstein, B. (1996) *Pedagogy, Symbolic Control and Identity*. London: Taylor and Francis.

BASIL BERNSTEIN

Remembrances

Susan F. Semel, Associate Professor of Education,
Hofstra University, Hempstead, NY

I FIRST MET Basil Bernstein during his visit to Adelphi University in 1987, where he delivered the Finkelstein Lecture, which became his 'Social class and pedagogic practice' chapter in *Class, Codes and Control, Volume 4*. At the time, I saw an immediate relationship to my own work on the history of progressive education in the United States. Since 1987, Basil and I became friends and we continued our ongoing conversation about the relationship between social class and progressive practice.

I have used a number of his works, including 'On the classification and framing of educational knowledge',[1] 'Class and pedagogies: visible and invisible',[2] 'Social class and pedagogic practice',[3] *Class, Codes and Control, Volume 3*,[4] *Pedagogy, Symbolic Control and Identity*,[5] and Bernstein's response to my chapter on his work in A.R. Sadovnik's *Knowledge and Pedagogy: The Sociology of Basil Bernstein*[6] to provide a sociological theory that explains my own histories of progressive education and schools, as well as my own experiences in a progressive school, first as a transfer student from a traditional public school and second, as a teacher in the same progressive school. His work on the social class basis of invisible pedagogy has been invaluable in explaining the social class basis of American progressive education and the difficulties working-class students often have reading elaborated codes.

The most important part of Bernstein's work is its ability to provide a theoretical model for understanding the processes of schooling. I have been, however, critical of code theory's placing primary emphasis on social class, which often places gender in a secondary position. Although Bernstein responded to this criticism by me and others in *Knowledge and Pedagogy* by stating that gender has been a crucial component of his theory, I am still less convinced than he was. Bernstein's response to my work on US progressive education, nonetheless, has provided me with an important analysis of the conditions necessary for progressive education to work for working class and low income students.

I have used Bernstein's theory of pedagogic practice to analyse the history of progressive education in the United States. I have argued in a number of publications that Bernstein's theory that progressive education (particularly invisible pedagogy) is the pedagogy of the upper middle class has been supported by the historical evidence in the US.[7] I have also argued that Bernstein's work is limited in helping us to understand why women were so instrumental in founding and running these early progressive schools (although Bernstein argues in response that his theory provides an explanation of such gender differences).

Finally, my most recent work uses Bernstein's work to examine empirically whether progressive education for low-income children in schools such as Central Park East Secondary School and Urban Academy in New York City disadvantages these students as Lisa Delpit suggests such schools often do. I have used Bernstein's work because it provides a sociological theory that frames my own historical descriptions. As a historian of education, I had resisted social theory and up until my reading of Bernstein agreed with the dictum of my mentor, Lawrence Cremin, that good history embeds its analysis in the narrative. After reading Bernstein, however, I came to the conclusion that sociological theory can provide an important frame to understand historical narrative. Since 1992, I have relied heavily on sociological theory in general, and Bernstein in particular, to make sense of my historical research.

Following Bernstein's response to my article in which he argued that code theory has a gender component, I went back and reread the sections in *Class, Codes and Control, Volume 3* that he cited (in a personal communication), as well as chapters by Arnot and Delamont in *Knowledge and Pedagogy*. I still believe that although Bernstein's work privileges social class, code theory does connect well to feminist theory, particularly with respect to how women have been historically engaged in the pedagogy of the family (i.e. socialization) and how middle-class women were instrumental in the creation of progressive education both in the US and UK. For example, Arnot, David and Wiener's recent work shows how the Victorian ideology of 'romance' for women has been central to women's gender roles, albeit differentially defined for middle-class and working-class women.

In addition to his scholarship, Basil was an exemplary teacher. I will never forget Basil's willingness to participate in our summer programme at the Institute of Education. Even when his health was failing, he tried to come and lecture to our students and help them make sense of what they were seeing in the London schools. In 1995, his last lecture to our students, he was remarkable. The class simply loved him and incorporated many of his insights into their field research papers. Like all great teachers, Basil met them at their intellectual level and helped to raise them up to his own. Although this was not possible, he did have a profound effect on their thinking; many of them still talk about it years later.

Although Basil had a significant influence on my work, the Basil I will most miss is Basil, the friend. Over the past ten years, Alan Sadovnik and I have shared many special times with Basil and Marion: dinner at their home in Dulwich, and at a number of his favourite restaurants in London, including the North Sea Fish Restaurant, Isolabella, and Chez Gerard; performances in the West End and at the National Theatre; and discussions about art. Most of all, Basil and I shared a passion for shopping, that neither Alan nor Marion shared. Basil and I would delight at going to the July sales at Harrods, Liberty's, Harvey Nichols, and up and down Bond Street. I will never forget one wonderful day at Monsoon, where Basil the teacher told me, his student, 'Darling heart, you have to accessorize that dress.'

When we saw Basil last in June 2000, after the Lisbon conference on his work, I knew it might well be the final time. Unfortunately, it was. A few days after his death, Alan and I were preparing for dinner, still saddened by the news. We went downstairs and bought one of his favourites, a vintage Chianti Classico, and during dinner toasted Basil and remembered all of the good times we had with him and Marion. I miss him terribly and will always cherish Basil Bernstein, pre-eminent sociologist and wonderful friend.

Notes

1 In M.F.D. Young, *Knowledge and Control: New directions for the sociology of education* (London: Collier-Macmillan, 1971).

2 Revised edition, in B. Bernstein, *Class, Codes and Control: Vol. 3* (London: Routledge and Kegan Paul, 1977: 116–56).

3 In B. Bernstein, *Class, Codes and Control: Vol. 4* (London: Routledge, 1990).

4 (London: Routledge and Kegan Paul, 1975).

5 (London: Taylor and Francis, 1996).

6 (Norwood, NJ: Ablex Publishing Corporation, 1995: 337–58).

7 See S.F. Semel, *The Dalton School: The Transformation of a Progressive School* (New York: Lang, 1992); S.F. Semel, 'Bernstein's theory of pedagogic practice: applications to the history of progressive education in the United States', in A.R. Sadovnik (ed.) *Knowledge and Pedagogy: The sociology of Basil Bernstein* (Norwood, NJ: Ablex, 1995: 337–58); S.F. Semel and A.R. Sadovnik, 'Lessons from the past: individualism and community in three progressive schools' *Peabody Journal of Education* (1995) 70 (4): 56–85; S.F. Semel and A.R. Sadovnik 'Schools of Tomorrow,' *Schools of Today: What happened to progressive education?* (New York: Lang, 1999); A.R. Sadovnik and S.F. Semel, 'Durkheim, Dewey and progressive education: the tensions between individualism and community', in W. Pickering and G. Walford (eds) *Durkheim on Education* (London: Routledge, 1998).

BASIL BERNSTEIN

'A sociology for the transmission of knowledges'

Parlo Singh, Centre for Language, Literacy and Diversity,
Queensland University of Technology

The intellectual field is ... a place to appropriate positions, to market approaches, to control the production and circulation of texts. From this point of view ... academics and practitioners established their ideological purity by distancing themselves from my work. I legitimated them by my own defaults. Those for whom the work had significance, use value rather than exchange value, found it relevant to their research.

(Bernstein 1995: 397)

THE USE VALUE of Basil Bernstein's theoretical and empirical research to the discipline of sociology of knowledge should not be underestimated. He was a brilliant and highly original thinker, researcher and teacher. Over four decades of research, he explored difficult educational questions relating to the (re)production of social inequality through schooling institutions. As Michael Halliday has argued, the question that Bernstein set out to answer was as follows: 'Given that (a) native wit is not determined by social class, and (b) all children now receive equivalent basic schooling, why are those children who *fail* to become educated almost all from the lower working class? (Halliday 1995: 127).

This is the same question that sociologists of education struggle to answer today. However, what set Bernstein apart from many of his contemporaries was his preoccupation 'with devices of transmission, relays of the symbolic, modalities of practice, and the construction and change of forms of consciousness' (1995: 392). He argued that 'the particular form a social relation takes acts selectively on what is said, when it said and how it is said' (1971: 123). It is through this social relation that a child acquires a specific social identity and orientation to meaning. Thus, Bernstein (1981) was fundamentally concerned with analysing the social or pedagogic relation between transmitter and acquirer.

Bernstein's analytic brilliance came through his theorization of power and control relations. According to Bernstein (1996) relations of symbolic control refer to *who* controls *what* in the pedagogic relation. Thus relations of control constitute legitimate forms of communication for different categories of agents (i.e., teacher–student, different categories of students), discourses (different categories of knowledge) and contexts (i.e., spaces within the school). Principles of control carry the boundary relations of power and socialize individuals into these relations. Power relations refer to the strength of the insulation of the boundaries between categories of agents, discourses and institutional contexts. Through relations of power, the categories of persons who interact in pedagogic communication, in addition to the categories of discourses transmitted in these interactions, and the categories of institutional contexts are constituted. In other words,

> power relations ... create boundaries, legitimize boundaries, reproduce boundaries, between different categories of groups, gender, class, race, different categories of discourse, different categories of agents. Thus power always operates to produce dislocations, to produce punctuations in social space.
> (Bernstein 1996: 19)

In this way, power relations establish legitimate relations of social order.

In undertaking and/or supervising empirical work, Bernstein examined social processes in four stages. First he concentrated on the 'control system, then on the boundaries it sets up, then on the ideological justifications which come to surround those boundaries, and finally on the power which underlies the whole system/process' (Delamont 1995: 324). In this way, Bernstein attempted to explain the link between power and control relations constituting pedagogic relations at the micro level of teacher–student interactions, for example, and the macro level of official state (policy) discourses.

In his attempt to grapple with changes in symbolic forms and the constitution of new subject positions, Bernstein (1986; 1990; 1996; 1999; 2000) developed a sophisticated model of pedagogic discourse (see also Bernstein and Diaz 1984; Christie 1999; Rose 1999). Principally, Bernstein proposed that schooling institutions transmit specialized forms of discourse, namely pedagogic discourse. Recontextualizing agents, such as syllabus writers and classroom teachers select, from contexts outside of schooling institutions, two types of discourses, instructional discourse (ID) and regulative discourse (RD), to produce a specific discourse (pedagogic discourse). The instructional discourse is always incorporated or embedded in the regulative discourse, such that the latter dominates the former. Instructional discourse is the knowledge that is selected and organized for the purposes of teaching and learning. Regulative discourse establishes the order within the instructional discourse. It generates principles of selection, organization, pacing and criteria of skills, concepts and information (i.e., the arbitrary internal ordering of school knowledge). It also deploys theories of instruction, and thus contains within itself 'a model of the learner and of the teacher and of the relation' between teacher and learner (Bernstein 1996: 49). Thus the specialized mode of social interaction or communication between teacher and student – that is, whole-class teacher monologue, triadic dialogue (teacher question, student response, teacher evaluation) and seatwork activities – are constituted by the regulative discourses. However, the model of the learner, teacher and teacher–student communication 'is never wholly utilitarian; it contains ideological elements' (Bernstein 1996: 49). Thus regulative discourses perform a crucial ideological function because they conceal the relations of power and control generating the arbitrary internal ordering of school knowledge.

Bernstein insisted on the importance of making explicit the models, theories and/or languages of description used to: define a research problem, produce data, analyse and interpret data, and write up this data. He argued

> we all have models – some are more explicit than others; we all use principles of descriptions – again some are more explicit than others; we all set up criteria to enable us to produce for ourselves, and to read the descriptions of others – again these criteria may vary in their explicitness. Some of our principles may be quantitative whilst others are qualitative. But the problem is fundamentally the same. In the end whose voice is speaking? My preference is to be explicit as possible. Then at least my voice may be deconstructed.
> (Bernstein 1996: 129)

References

Bernstein, B. (1971) *Class, Codes and Control: Vol 1*. London: Routledge and Kegan Paul.

Bernstein, B. (1975) *Class, Codes and Control: Vol 3*. London: Routledge and Kegan Paul.

Bernstein, B. (1981) 'Codes, modalities and the process of cultural reproduction: a model', *Language and Society* 10: 327–63.

Bernstein, B. (1986) 'On pedagogic discourse', in J.G. Richardson (ed.) *Handbook of Theory and Research for the Sociology of Education*. New York: Greenwood Press.

Bernstein, B. (1990) *Class, Codes and Control: Vol. 4: The Structure of Pedagogic Discourse*. London: Routledge.

Bernstein, B. (1995) 'Response', in A.R. Sadovnik (ed.) *Pedagogy and Knowledge: The sociology of Basil Bernstein*. Norwood, NJ: Ablex.

Bernstein, B. (1996) *Pedagogy, Symbolic Control and Identity: Theory, research, critique.* London: Taylor and Francis.

Bernstein, B. (1999) 'Vertical and horizontal discourse: an essay, *British Journal of Sociology of Education* 20 (2): 157–74.

Bernstein, B. (2000) 'From pedagogies to knowledges', in A. Morais (ed.) *Towards a Sociology of Pedagogy: The contribution of Basil Bernstein to research.* University of Lisbon: School of Science, Department of Education and Centre for Educational Research.

Bernstein, B. and Diaz, M. (1984) 'Towards a theory of pedagogic discourse', Collected Original Resources in Education, *CORE*, 8, 3.

Christie, F. (ed.) (1999) *Pedagogy and the Shaping of Consciousness: Linguistic and social processes.* London: Continuum.

Delamont, S. (1995) 'Bernstein and the analysis of gender inequality: considerations and applications', in A.R. Sadovnik (ed.) *Pedagogy and Knowledge: The Sociology of Basil Bernstein.* Norwood, NJ: Ablex: 323–6.

Halliday, M.A.K. (1995) 'Language and the theory of codes', in A.R. Sadovnik (ed.) *Pedagogy and Knowledge: The sociology of Basil Bernstein.* Norwood, NJ: Ablex: 127–44.

Rose, D. (1999) 'Culture, competence and schooling: approaches to literacy teaching in indigenous school education', in F. Christie (eds) *Pedagogy and the Shaping of Consciousness.* London: Continuum.

BASIL BERNSTEIN

A tribute

Barbara Tizard, Emeritus Professor of Education,
Institute of Education, University of London

As I am not a sociologist, I can only write of Basil as a friend and colleague. I first met him in the late sixties. My husband, Jack, had been appointed to a new Chair in Child Development at the Institute of Education, and found Basil much the cleverest and most 'sympathique' of his fellow professors. Coming from the Institute of Psychiatry, an intellectual hothouse, Jack was appalled at the intellectual apathy then prevalent in many departments. He and Basil worked together to raise the status of research in the Institute, and indeed to try to turn it into a research-based institution. Basil in particular always fought to improve the conditions of employment, including job security, of research staff. He also played a leading role within the University on those political issues he felt strongly that academics should take up, particularly racism and the threat at that time to Chilean academics and students.

Basil quickly became a family friend. His iconoclasm, high spirits, and the warmth of his interest in them impressed even my teenage children, who tended to scorn our friends. He was an equal success with the younger children, on one occasion delighting them by impersonating a sheep, crawling, baa-ing round the living room, with his sheepskin jacket put on inside out. He won me over, the first time I met him, at a party, by asking really detailed questions about my research, suggesting possible future leads, and arguing the merits of his own theoretical framework. His eyes lit up as he sparked with ideas, and this intellectual enthusiasm never left him – even in the last days of his life he could summon the energy to discuss a project. He would discuss psychology as readily as sociology, being genuinely interested in, and sympathetic towards it, an interest he had developed even before meeting Marion, his wife, who is a clinical psychologist.

It was, however, after my husband died in 1979, and I succeeded him as Director of the Thomas Coram Research Unit, that I saw much more of Basil. Until then a back room researcher, I knew little of the decision-making processes and the strategy of operating within the complex networks of large institutions. The glory days of social science research, when funds were easy to obtain, were rapidly passing, and the former power of Institute professors had been largely removed. Basil, because he valued research, and from friendship, provided the support I needed. He appointed himself as unofficial protector of the Unit in the Institute, fighting for its interest – and the interest of other Institute researchers at every level. Committee work, which I found terminally boring, delighted him. He regarded every meeting as a challenge, a kind of battle, which with the right strategy and tactics he could win. He would attend a meeting with clear aims, carefully laid plans and chosen allies, whom he charmed and flattered. To opponents, and those he believed to be critics of his work, he could be cuttingly hostile. He never feared, and too often succeeded in, making enemies. He was secretive, undoubtedly prickly and oversensitive, given to mercurial and unpredictable mood changes, but at his best warm, funny and generous.

However, what was most important about Basil, and to him, was his contribution to the sociology of education. His passion for grand theory set him apart from the main stream of British social science researchers. He, in return, despised empirical work that did not have a theoretical base. But he also believed that theories needed to be supported by empirical data. He regarded his own empirical research, much of which was done with postgraduate students, as crucial to his theory, and was constantly irritated that it tended to be neglected. He was even more irritated that he was generally known only for his early work on elaborated and restricted codes, rather than for his continuously evolving model of the symbolic structures of educational power and control. The fact that non-sociologists, including myself, often found his later writings difficult to understand was a further source of annoyance, although he gradually came to accept it – on a copy of his latest book he wrote for me 'Not for reading, only for friendship'.

I watched Basil's retirement anxiously. He had interests outside work – he was a hi-fi enthusiast, in a small way a patron of the arts, and a talented photographer – but it was his work that was central to his identity. True, he could continue to supervise postgraduate students, mostly from overseas, to whom he was very generous with his time and support. He also continued to write and edit, and until his final illness he went into his office on most days. But he mourned his loss of power – he was no longer one of the three most powerful people in the Institute, whom many feared and everyone listened to

– and the stimulation and excitement he drew from committee work. Suddenly, despite his continuing international distinction and academic productivity, he found himself outside the main Institute, in a room little bigger than a cupboard, and virtually isolated. He told me he felt that he was a ghost, that he had become invisible. But it was also the case that he himself avoided ex-colleagues.

At times, he became very angry with me, for periods of weeks or months. At other times we met for lunch in his office most weeks, which barely held two people, sharing smoked salmon sandwiches and coffee ceremoniously made in his cafetière, or when he was in an ebullient mood, in a nearby Italian restaurant. Basil was no Puritan. He liked to spend money on good food, wine and expensive clothes, and it was hard for him as his illness set in to limit his diet and give up wine and later coffee. Over lunch we discussed our work, and, increasingly his health, and gossiped. Gradually over the years he overcame his initial depression and anger at having to retire, and became reconciled to this new life, even seeing merits in his tiny room. He was helped by the large number of invitations to lecture he continued to receive from overseas universities (he would insist on first-class travel) and by the six honorary degrees bestowed on him, two after his retirement. Although he continued to feel resentful that his work had never been adequately acknowledged in this country, or at the Institute, he did realize that his influence had been far reaching. Death was very unwelcome to him, and despite pain, he fought for his life. Like many others, I feel a great loss at the death of this gifted, complex, larger than life friend and colleague.

BASIL BERNSTEIN

An Australian tribute

Geoff Williams, President,
Australian Systemic Functional Linguistics Association

A FEW HOURS prior to this meeting there has been a parallel seminar in Sydney to celebrate Basil's life and work, and to discuss recent Australian research which draws on his theoretical insights in seeking a sociological explanation of linguistic variation. The event was convened by the Australian Systemic Functional Linguistics Association and it is the first occasion on which the association has honoured a scholar in this way.

That Bernstein's work did not always attract the high regard of linguists is well-known so it may be a little surprising to hear that a linguistics association in another continent has arranged such a tribute. Bernstein's own comments about his relations with linguists in 'Sociolinguistics: a personal view' (1996) are some of his most wryly amusing and pointed, which is, of course, to say very pointed indeed. He seems to have delighted in quoting the famous linguist who considered his theory to be 'below rationality'. However, fortunately he did maintain a close dialogue with many linguists, most notably with Michael Halliday and Ruqaiya Hasan. In his 1996 work Bernstein comments that '[their] contribution to my development is incalculable' (1996: 149). Both Halliday and Hasan have similarly acknowledged the influence of Bernstein's work on the social aspects of their theory of language as social semiotic (e.g. Halliday 1976: 24ff.; Hasan 1973, 1996).

Halliday and Hasan arrived in Sydney in 1976, and very soon afterwards their Australian colleagues were included in conversations about the social and the linguistic. Bernstein made his first visit to Australia in 1978 and by the early 1980s linguistic research that was directly influenced by his theory of coding orientation was published by Hasan. In 1996 Bernstein was again able to accept an invitation to a conference, having been forced to abandon plans for earlier visits by health difficulties. Papers from the 1996 conference, which was devoted exclusively to interaction between his sociological theory and systemic functional linguistics, were published as *Pedagogy and the Shaping of Consciousness* (1999), edited by the conference convenor, Frances Christie. In the years between Bernstein's two visits, developments in Australian work in systemic functional linguistics owed much to his own further theoretical moves. Two major fields of research have been produced: in educational linguistics on implicit/explicit pedagogy and writing development; and in language variation theory, a specific theory of semantic variation.

Educational linguistics in Australia has been heavily influenced by Bernstein's insights into the structuring social relations through which curricula are produced and achieve their reproductive effects. The best known of these projects took as its starting point an effect of what Bernstein termed 'pernicious localization'. By making extensive linguistic analyses James Martin, Joan Rothery, Frances Christie and others were able to show how schools required children to produce specific genres of written text without regard to the distribution rules creating differential access to privileged text types in local pedagogies. These scholars and their colleagues subsequently developed an explicit pedagogy, based sociologically on classification and framing theory and linguistically on an expansion of register theory. The linguistic descriptions of privileging text types and the model for writing pedagogy have influenced curricula in Australia, Hong Kong, Singapore, Scandinavia and, of course, more recently England. Significantly, the sociological theory both enables the development of, and *also anticipates the reception of,* the pedagogic intervention into social class relations. I don't know whether Martin and his colleagues were as aware at that time as they are now of Bernstein's concept of recontextualization, but his analysis of the likely reshaping of ideas as they move from the field of production into a field of pedagogic reproduction uncannily predicts the use of this research by the New South Wales government. I understand this may also now be the case in the English context.

The second example of research originated in early work in the Sociological Research Unit but the empirical work and enabling linguistic theory continue to be developed in Sydney by Ruqaiya Hasan and her colleagues. Its particular focus is the issue that preoccupied Bernstein in so much of his theoretical exploration: how the outside becomes the inside and how the inside reveals itself and shapes the outside. This work has involved two dimensions: from the linguistic point of view, making intensive analyses of extensive examples of naturally occurring talk in order to explore the variable selection of semantic features by people in contrasted social positions; and from the social perspective, expanding accounts of the theoretical interface between the social and the linguistic. The 'social' aspect is exemplified by Hasan's critique of Bourdieu's position on the social and the linguistic, Cloran's elaboration of the concept of decontextualized language, and Williams' work on the pedagogic device and variants of local pedagogic discourse.

One of the features of Bernstein's sociological work that has made it so particularly attractive to linguists has been the depth of his appreciation of the theoretical relations involved. In his 1996 work he commented:

> Very complex questions are raised by the relation of the socio to the linguistic. What linguistic theories of description are available for what socio issues? And how do the former limit the latter? What determines the dynamics of the linguistic theory, and how do these dynamics relate, if at all, to the dynamics of change in those disciplines which do and could contribute to the socio. If 'socio' and linguistics are to illuminate language as a truly social construct, then there must be mutually translatable principles of descriptions which enable the dynamics of the social to enter those translatable principles. (1996: 151–2)

We read here both Bernstein's interest in substantive questions about language, but also his interest in producing theoretically elegant relations, a feature notably absent from so much other work on social class and language use. This concern for elegance he shared with Hasan in both the theoretical and empirical work on semantic variation.

I conclude with a brief comment on Bernstein's personal relations with Australian colleagues. Bernstein was, of course, a generous correspondent, and tucked into the private files of several researchers may be found handwritten letters of encouragement from him. However, in the 'Basil' folders of the emails are also to be found messages populated liberally with question marks and without the pleasant epithets of the handwritten notes. These messages are about the yet-to-be-voiced, particularly about the enduring questions of relations between micro encounters and macro contexts. They typically end with the invitation, 'Let's keep in contact about this.' The Australian seminar today indicates our vigorous intention to keep his sociological contributions in contact with linguistic theory in order to continue the critical dialogue.

On behalf of the Australian Systemic Functional Linguistics Association and Bernstein's close colleagues in sociology in Australia, several of whom have also participated in the Sydney seminar, I wish you well for the London celebrations and discussions.

References

Bernstein, B. (1996) 'Socioloinguistics: a personal view', in *Pedagogy, Symbolic Control and identity: Theory, research, critique*. London: Taylor and Francis.

Christie, F. (ed.) (1999) *Pedagogy and the Shaping of Consciousness: Linguistic and social processes*. London: Cassell.

Halliday, M.A.K. (1976) *Language as Social Semiotic*. London: Edward Arnold.

Hasan, R. (1973) 'Code, register and social dialect', in B. Bernstein, *Class, Codes and Control: Vol. 2: Applied Studies towards a Sociology of Language*. London: Routledge and Kegan Paul.

Hasan, R. (1996) *Ways of Saying, Ways of Meaning: Selected papers of Ruqaiya Hasan*. Edited by C. Cloran, D. Butt and G. Williams. London: Cassell.

BASIL BERNSTEIN

A personal appreciation

Michael Young, Professor of Education,
Lifelong Learning, Institute of Education,
University of London

I FIRST MET Basil Bernstein when I was an MA student at Essex University in 1966. The effect of his seminars on me, and others I am sure, was electric and a revelation about what sociology of education might involve that went far beyond anything we could have found in a book or journal. We came to his seminars full of enthusiasm for sociological theory (mostly American) that we imagined could be 'applied' to education. However, Bernstein had quite other ideas; he saw education as a social phenomenon in its own right and as a source of theories about society. For him, the task of the sociologist was not to apply theories to education that had been developed elsewhere but to make explicit the ways in which educational institutions exemplified features of the society of which they were a part. In this way sociology of education not only offered a fresh and more objective view of educational problems but could address the more fundamental issues about the nature of society. Bernstein saw that who we are and who we become and how societies are made and changed are all influenced in important ways by institutions like the school and by processes like pedagogy and assessment.

I sometimes used to travel to London with Basil after the Essex seminars and on a number of occasions he invited me back to his home in Dulwich. We would talk late into the night in what was both a continuing conversation and for me an extended tutorial. It was during these talks that he made two suggestions that were to shape the rest of my professional life. First he encouraged me to apply for a lectureship in sociology of education at the Institute of Education, something I had not dreamed of considering. Second, he introduced me to the idea that it was the curriculum – the very stuff of education

– that should be at the centre of the sociology of education. The curriculum was the topic of my MA dissertation and has been at the centre of my research interests ever since.

The story of how my book, *Knowledge and Control*, came about tells much of Bernstein's generosity to a junior colleague with his academic reputation still to make. He encouraged me to present a paper on the sociology of the curriculum to the 1970 Annual Conference of the British Sociological Association. When it was clear that the official collection of conference papers was not going to generate the new directions for the sociology of education that he thought were important, it was Bernstein who suggested that I should edit a book that would sharpen the issues. The idea for a book took shape after the conference in the bar of the Russell Hotel in a conversation between Bernstein, Pierre Bourdieu (who had also spoken at the conference) and me. Bernstein not only encouraged me to edit the book but agreed that his own paper should be included and helped me find a publisher. Furthermore, despite his own strong views and the fact that he was far from sympathetic to the book's eclectic and somewhat relativist approach to knowledge and the curriculum, he made no attempt to influence its content or my editorial direction.

Sociology of education in the 1970s was dominated by the debate, which seemed all-important to many of us at the time, between the 'old' and the 'new' sociologies of education. It was Basil Bernstein who pointed out that the debate could be understood not only in its own terms but, sociologically, as an example of generational conflict within the academic community. It was not until two decades later, when confronted with the extreme relativism of contemporary post-modernists that I recognized the importance of his insight that theoretical debates have their place but not as ends in themselves.

The sociology of education would be infinitely poorer without the contributions of Basil Bernstein. Everyone's list will vary; for me it was his continued affirmation of the importance of Emile Durkheim, especially at a time when he was widely if mistakenly dismissed as a functionalist, his emphasis on the creative as well as the constraining role of boundaries in the development of new knowledge and his conviction, long before it was 'discovered' by sociologists of science, that the social character of knowledge (and therefore the curriculum) did not undermine its objectivity; on the contrary, it is the condition for it.

Basil Bernstein's legacy will continue to be felt in many different intellectual fields. For those of us who met him and worked with him, this legacy will relate as much to him as a person as to his writings. He and I had our differences and sadly we spoke little in recent years. However, I shall always regard it as a privilege that I was taught by him and worked with him as a colleague. In particular, I shall remember his continuing ability to ask the important educational questions, his scepticism about anything that seemed like an intellectual fashion and his willingness to take the ideas of others seriously. Finally, there is something that I am sure will stay with many of us; even a decade after he retired and when he was already far from well, Basil Bernstein never thought his job was done; he never gave up tackling the most fundamental educational problems faced by modern societies.

A final thought. Bernstein was an extremely complex person but always, for me, a radical at heart. However, he had the courage as well as the insight to know that even for radicals there are things which it is important to conserve.